HORRORES OCULTOS

―――――◆―――――

Exponiendo el Abuso a los Ancianos y Protegiendo a Nuestros Seres Queridos

Autores

Danish Ali Bajwa y Usama Bajwa

Derechos de autor © 2023 por RK Books Publication

El contenido contenido en este libro no puede ser reproducido, duplicado o transmitido en ninguna forma o sistema de recuperación conocido actualmente o por inventarse en el futuro sin el permiso escrito directo del autor o editor. En ningún caso se responsabilizará al editor o autor por ningún daño, reparación o pérdida económica debida a la información contenida en este libro, ya sea directa o indirectamente.

Aviso legal:

Este libro está protegido por derechos de autor. Este libro es solo para uso personal. No puede modificar, distribuir, vender, usar, citar o parafrasear ninguna parte del contenido de este libro sin el consentimiento del autor o editor. "Uso Justo" implica un resumen o cita con el crédito apropiado al autor.

Aviso de exención de responsabilidad:

Tenga en cuenta que la información contenida en este libro es solo para fines educativos. Se ha realizado todo esfuerzo para presentar información precisa, actualizada, confiable y completa. No se hacen declaraciones ni implicaciones de garantía de ningún tipo. Los lectores reconocen que el autor no está proporcionando asesoramiento legal, financiero, médico o profesional. El contenido de este libro se ha derivado de diversas fuentes. Consulte a un profesional calificado antes de intentar cualquier técnica descrita en este libro. Al leer y usar este libro, el lector acepta que en ningún caso el autor será responsable de las pérdidas directas o indirectas incurridas debido al uso de la información en este libro, incluyendo, pero no limitándose a, errores, omisiones o inexactitudes.

Correo electrónico: rkbooks16@gmail.com

ISBN del libro electrónico: 978-969-3492-42-2

ISBN del libro en rústica: 978-969-3492-43-9

ISBN del libro en tapa dura: 978-969-3492-44-6

Biografía del autor

Danish Ali Bajwa y Usama Bajwa, conocidos conjuntamente como los Hermanos Bajwa, forman un dinámico dúo de escritores conocido por su amplia gama de obras publicadas que abarcan varios géneros. Nacidos y criados en un hogar donde la creatividad y el conocimiento eran altamente valorados, estos hermanos aprovecharon su innato talento para contar historias y explorar en una próspera carrera en la literatura.

Danish Ali Bajwa es un prolífico escritor con una habilidad única para conectar con una audiencia diversa. Con una voz distintiva, ha contribuido a una extensa colección de libros infantiles, donde entrelaza con elegancia lecciones de vida esenciales con narrativas cautivadoras que resuenan en las mentes jóvenes. Más allá de la literatura infantil, el portafolio de Usama también incluye varios libros de motivación. Tiene una habilidad sorprendente para elevar e inspirar a los lectores a través de sus narrativas convincentes y representaciones auténticas del espíritu humano. Las palabras de Usama sirven como un faro de positividad, inspirando a los lectores a conquistar sus miedos y alcanzar su verdadero potencial.

Por otro lado, Usama Bajwa aporta una perspectiva analítica a su colaboración escrita. Con un gran interés en la intersección entre los negocios y la tecnología, Danish ha escrito varios libros informativos, haciendo que temas complejos sean accesibles y atractivos para los lectores. La experiencia de Danish en temas relacionados con los negocios y la tecnología es evidente en sus guías completas e intuitivas. Sobresale en presentar ideas innovadoras y tendencias futuristas con una comprensión fundamentada en las necesidades empresariales contemporáneas, convirtiendo sus libros en una referencia en las bibliotecas de emprendedores ambiciosos y entusiastas de la tecnología.

Juntos, Danish y Usama han cultivado un estilo de escritura único y diverso que cautiva a sus lectores, manteniéndolos absortos desde la primera hasta la última página. Sus libros a menudo reflejan la simbiosis de sus diferentes intereses y experiencia, y el poderoso equilibrio entre la emoción y la lógica. A pesar de sus variados intereses, comparten el compromiso de crear literatura de alta calidad que sea a la vez cautivadora e iluminadora. Los Hermanos Bajwa continúan estableciendo su presencia en el mundo literario, construyendo un legado de libros perspicaces, provocadores y encantadores que realmente marcan la diferencia.

PREFACIO

En los rincones silenciosos de nuestra sociedad, persiste un problema siniestro y omnipresente: el abuso a los ancianos. Tras puertas cerradas, los adultos mayores son sometidos a diversas formas de maltrato, su confianza es violada y su bienestar comprometido. Es un asunto profundamente angustiante que exige nuestra atención, empatía y acción colectiva. Este libro, "Horrores Ocultos: Exponiendo el Abuso a los Ancianos y Protegiendo a Nuestros Seres Queridos", tiene como objetivo arrojar luz sobre esta oscura realidad, desentrañar sus complejidades y brindar perspectivas para proteger a nuestra población en envejecimiento.

Dentro de las páginas de este libro, emprendemos un viaje de comprensión y defensa. Nos adentramos en las diferentes formas de abuso a los ancianos, que van desde el abuso físico y emocional hasta la explotación financiera y el abandono. Al examinar estas formas, esperamos ampliar nuestra perspectiva y profundizar nuestra conciencia sobre los desafíos que enfrentan los adultos mayores.

Si bien el abuso a los ancianos puede parecer oculto, las señales suelen estar presentes, esperando ser reconocidas. Este libro se esfuerza por equipar a los lectores con el conocimiento y las herramientas para identificar las señales de alerta y tomar medidas adecuadas. Exploramos los indicadores de abuso: lesiones físicas, cambios repentinos en el comportamiento, aislamiento social e irregularidades financieras, en un esfuerzo por capacitar a los lectores para que estén vigilantes y respondan a las necesidades de sus seres queridos.

Para abordar el problema de manera efectiva, es crucial comprender los complejos factores que contribuyen al abuso a los ancianos. Nos adentramos en las dinámicas sociales e individuales que subyacen a estos actos, explorando el edadismo, el estrés de los cuidadores, el aislamiento social y la falta de conciencia y recursos como factores clave que contribuyen. Al arrojar luz sobre estos factores, esperamos estimular una comprensión más profunda de las causas subyacentes e inspirar la acción en múltiples niveles.

No basta con simplemente reconocer las señales y comprender los factores que contribuyen; también debemos trabajar juntos para crear una sociedad donde se prevenga y aborde el abuso a los ancianos de manera efectiva. Este libro profundiza en la importancia de la participación comunitaria, los marcos legales y los cambios sistémicos en el cuidado de los ancianos. Exploramos la importancia de construir redes de apoyo sólidas, fomentar conexiones intergeneracionales y abogar por cambios en las políticas para proteger los derechos y el bienestar de los adultos mayores.

Además, abordamos el papel crítico de los cuidadores en la prevención y el abordaje del abuso a los ancianos. Los cuidadores tienen una inmensa responsabilidad e influencia en la vida de los adultos mayores, y es esencial proporcionarles el apoyo y los recursos necesarios para brindar cuidados de calidad mientras salvaguardan la dignidad de quienes están a su cargo. Hablamos sobre el agotamiento de los cuidadores, la gestión del estrés y los programas de capacitación que pueden equipar a los cuidadores con las habilidades y la resiliencia necesarias para enfrentar los desafíos que puedan surgir.

A lo largo de este libro, enfatizamos la importancia de la educación, la conciencia y la defensa. Al difundir el conocimiento, crear conciencia y participar en esfuerzos de defensa, podemos trabajar colectivamente hacia un futuro donde se erradique el abuso a los ancianos y los adultos mayores puedan envejecer con dignidad, respeto y la calidad de vida que merecen. Hacemos un llamado a los lectores para que se unan a nosotros en este importante esfuerzo, ya que cada individuo tiene un papel que desempeñar en la protección de nuestros seres queridos y en la construcción de una sociedad que valore y resguarde a su población en envejecimiento.

TABLE OF CONTENTS

Introducción; 1

Chapter 1 Understanding Elder Abuse: Defining the Problem . 4

Chapter 2 Recognizing the Signs: Identifying Abuse in Our Loved Ones 17

Chapter 3 The Profiles of Abusers: Unmasking the Perpetrators 33

Chapter 4 Unveiling the Dark Corners: Exploring Settings Prone to Abuse 45

Chapter 5 Breaking the Silence: Encouraging Reporting and Intervention 62

Chapter 6 Legal Frameworks: Understanding the Rights and Protections for Seniors 79

Chapter 7 Preventive Measures Safeguarding Our Loved Ones 96

Chapter 8 Empowering Caregivers: Training and Support for Quality Care 116

Chapter 9 Healing and Recovery: Rehabilitation for Abuse Survivors 134

Chapter 10 Creating a Brighter Future: Advocacy and Policy Changes 152

Conclusión 185

Introducción;

En los rincones silenciosos de nuestra sociedad, persiste un problema siniestro y omnipresente: el abuso a los ancianos. Tras puertas cerradas, los adultos mayores son sometidos a diversas formas de maltrato, su confianza es violada y su bienestar comprometido. Es un asunto profundamente angustiante que exige nuestra atención, empatía y acción colectiva. Este libro, "Horrores Ocultos: Exponiendo el Abuso a los Ancianos y Protegiendo a Nuestros Seres Queridos", tiene como objetivo arrojar luz sobre esta oscura realidad, desentrañar sus complejidades y brindar perspectivas para proteger a nuestra población en envejecimiento.

Dentro de las páginas de este libro, emprendemos un viaje de comprensión y defensa. Nos adentramos en las diferentes formas de abuso a los ancianos, que van desde el abuso físico y emocional hasta la explotación financiera y el abandono. Al examinar estas formas, esperamos ampliar nuestra perspectiva y profundizar nuestra conciencia sobre los desafíos que enfrentan los adultos mayores.

Si bien el abuso a los ancianos puede parecer oculto, las señales suelen estar presentes, esperando ser reconocidas. Este libro se esfuerza por equipar a los lectores con el conocimiento y las herramientas para identificar las señales de alerta y tomar medidas adecuadas. Exploramos los indicadores de abuso: lesiones físicas, cambios repentinos en el comportamiento, aislamiento social e irregularidades financieras, en un esfuerzo por capacitar a los lectores para que estén vigilantes y respondan a las necesidades de sus seres queridos.

Para abordar el problema de manera efectiva, es crucial comprender los complejos factores que contribuyen al abuso a los ancianos. Nos adentramos en las dinámicas sociales e individuales que subyacen a estos actos, explorando el edadismo, el estrés de los cuidadores, el aislamiento social y la falta de conciencia y recursos como factores clave que contribuyen. Al arrojar luz sobre estos factores, esperamos estimular una comprensión más profunda de las causas subyacentes e inspirar la acción en múltiples niveles.

No basta con simplemente reconocer las señales y comprender los factores que contribuyen; también debemos trabajar juntos para crear una sociedad donde se prevenga y aborde el abuso a los ancianos de manera efectiva. Este libro profundiza en la importancia de la participación comunitaria, los marcos legales y los cambios sistémicos en el cuidado de los ancianos. Exploramos la importancia de construir redes de apoyo sólidas, fomentar conexiones intergeneracionales y abogar por cambios en las políticas para proteger los derechos y el bienestar de los adultos mayores.

Además, abordamos el papel crítico de los cuidadores en la prevención y el abordaje del abuso a los ancianos. Los cuidadores tienen una inmensa responsabilidad e influencia en la vida de los adultos mayores, y es esencial proporcionarles el apoyo y los recursos necesarios para brindar cuidados de calidad mientras salvaguardan la dignidad de quienes están a su cargo. Hablamos sobre el agotamiento de los cuidadores, la gestión del estrés y los programas de capacitación que pueden equipar a los cuidadores con las habilidades y la resiliencia necesarias para enfrentar los desafíos que puedan surgir.

A lo largo de este libro, enfatizamos la importancia de la educación, la conciencia y la defensa. Al difundir el conocimiento, crear conciencia y participar en esfuerzos de defensa, podemos trabajar colectivamente hacia un futuro donde se erradique el abuso a los ancianos y los adultos mayores puedan envejecer con dignidad, respeto y la calidad de vida que merecen. Hacemos un llamado a los lectores para que se unan a nosotros en este importante esfuerzo, ya que cada individuo tiene un papel que desempeñar en la protección de nuestros seres queridos y en la construcción de una sociedad que valore y resguarde a su población en envejecimiento.

CHAPTER 1
Understanding Elder Abuse: Defining the Problem

Elder abuse is a pressing issue that demands our attention and action. In this chapter, we will delve into the complexities of elder abuse, examining its various forms, exploring the alarming statistics and prevalence, and analyzing the underlying factors that contribute to its occurrence. By understanding the problem at its core, we can begin to tackle it effectively and protect our elderly loved ones.

The Forms of Elder Abuse

Elder abuse encompasses a range of harmful actions and behaviors directed towards older adults. It includes physical abuse, which involves inflicting pain, injury, or physical restraint. Emotional abuse refers to acts that cause distress, humiliation, or psychological harm, such as isolation, verbal insults, or threats. Financial abuse involves the illegal or improper use of an elderly person's funds, assets, or property. Sexual abuse encompasses non-consensual sexual acts, coercion, or inappropriate behavior. Neglect, the failure to provide necessary care and support, is also a form of elder abuse.

The Magnitude of the Problem

The prevalence of elder abuse is deeply concerning. Statistics reveal that a significant number of older adults experience abuse in various settings, including their own homes, nursing homes, or other care facilities. However, it is essential to recognize that elder abuse is vastly underreported due to factors such as fear, shame, and dependency on the abuser. Estimates suggest that only a fraction of abuse cases are disclosed, painting a stark picture of the hidden horrors faced by many seniors.

Factors Contributing to Elder Abuse

To fully comprehend elder abuse, we must examine the factors that contribute to its occurrence. One factor is social isolation, as seniors who lack social connections are more vulnerable to abuse. Ageism, which perpetuates stereotypes and marginalizes older adults, also plays a role in enabling abuse. Caregiver stress is another significant factor, as the demands and pressures of caregiving can sometimes lead to abusive behaviors. Understanding these contributing factors helps us address the root causes and develop comprehensive solutions.

Social Isolation

Social isolation is a prevalent risk factor for elder abuse. Older adults who are socially isolated often lack the support networks necessary for intervention and protection. They may be more susceptible to manipulation and exploitation, making them easier targets for abusers. By recognizing the importance of social connections and implementing strategies to combat isolation, we can reduce the risk of abuse.

Ageism

Ageism perpetuates negative stereotypes and biases against older adults, leading to discrimination and marginalization. These attitudes can undermine the dignity and worth of seniors, making them more susceptible to abuse. By challenging ageist beliefs and promoting intergenerational understanding and respect, we can create a culture that values and protects the rights of older adults.

Caregiver Stress: Caregivers, whether family members or professionals, often face significant stress and burnout while providing care to older adults. The demands of caregiving, coupled with limited resources and support, can increase the risk of abusive behaviors. By implementing comprehensive caregiver support programs, including respite care, counseling, and education, we can alleviate caregiver stress and reduce the occurrence of abuse.

The Impact of Elder Abuse

Elder abuse has devastating consequences for the well-being of older adults. Victims may experience physical injuries, emotional trauma, financial ruin, and a decline in overall health. The effects can be long-lasting, eroding trust, self-esteem, and the ability to live independently. Recognizing the profound impact of abuse underscores the urgency of addressing this issue and providing support and resources for survivors.

Understanding the complexity of elder abuse is crucial in our quest to protect our loved ones. By comprehending the various forms of abuse, acknowledging the magnitude of the problem, and examining the contributing factors, we gain valuable insights into the dynamics at play. Armed with this knowledge, we can develop comprehensive strategies, raise awareness, and promote a culture of respect and dignity for older adults. In doing so, we take the first steps toward exposing the hidden horrors of elder abuse and safeguarding the well-being of our seniors.

Different forms of elder abuse

Elder abuse encompasses a range of harmful actions and behaviors directed towards older adults. Each form of elder abuse presents unique challenges and impacts the well-being and dignity of older individuals. In this section, we will explore the different forms of elder abuse in detail, shedding light on the nature of each and the detrimental effects they can have on the lives of seniors.

Physical Abuse

- Physical abuse involves the use of force that results in pain, injury, or physical harm to an elderly person. This form of abuse can manifest through hitting, slapping, pushing, restraining, or using excessive force during caregiving activities. Physical abuse can leave visible signs such as bruises, fractures, burns, or unexplained injuries. It not only causes immediate physical pain but also takes a toll on the mental and emotional well-being of older adults.

- The consequences of physical abuse can be severe, leading to chronic pain, disability, and a decline in overall health. Victims may experience heightened fear, anxiety, and a loss of trust in others. The impact of physical abuse can be both physical and psychological, causing long-term trauma and affecting the individual's quality of life.

Emotional and Psychological Abuse

- Emotional or psychological abuse involves behaviors that inflict emotional pain, distress, or anguish on an older person. This form of abuse is often characterized by threats, insults, intimidation, humiliation, or isolation. Perpetrators may exert control by manipulating the emotions, thoughts, and actions of the elderly person. Emotional abuse can be difficult to detect, as it leaves no physical marks, but its effects can be profoundly damaging.

- Older adults who experience emotional abuse may suffer from anxiety, depression, low self-esteem, and a sense of helplessness. They may withdraw from social activities, lose interest in previously enjoyed hobbies, and become socially isolated. The constant fear and stress associated with emotional abuse can erode the individual's mental well-being, leading to long-term psychological consequences.

Financial Abuse

- Financial abuse refers to the unauthorized or improper use of an elderly person's funds, assets, or property. It involves actions such as theft, fraud, coercion, undue influence, or exploitation. Perpetrators may manipulate the older adult into signing over financial control, misuse their bank accounts, or deceive them into giving away their assets. Financial abuse can lead to significant financial losses, leaving the victim in a vulnerable and precarious situation.

- The impact of financial abuse extends beyond monetary loss. Older adults who experience financial abuse may face financial insecurity, jeopardizing their ability to meet basic needs and maintain their independence. They may experience feelings of betrayal, loss of trust, and a sense of powerlessness. Financial abuse can also have long-term repercussions on the individual's financial well-being and quality of life.

Sexual Abuse

- Sexual abuse involves any non-consensual sexual contact, coercion, or inappropriate behavior towards an older adult. This form of abuse can occur in various settings, including nursing homes, care facilities, or within the context of relationships. Perpetrators may exploit the vulnerability or cognitive impairments of the older adult to engage in sexual acts without their consent.

- The consequences of sexual abuse on older adults are devastating. Victims may experience physical injuries, trauma, and profound emotional distress. The violation of boundaries and the erosion of personal autonomy can have long-lasting effects on the individual's self-esteem, trust, and ability to form healthy relationships.

Neglect

- Neglect refers to the failure to provide necessary care, support, or protection to an elderly person. It can manifest as a lack of adequate food, shelter, medical care, personal hygiene assistance, or emotional support. Neglect can be intentional or unintentional, resulting from caregiver stress, lack of resources, or inadequate training.

- The consequences of neglect can be dire, leading to a decline in physical health, malnutrition, untreated medical conditions, and an increased risk of accidents or injuries. Neglected older adults may experience feelings of abandonment, isolation, and neglect-related trauma. The lack of essential care and support undermines their well-being and compromises their safety.

Understanding the different forms of elder abuse is crucial in recognizing and addressing this grave issue. Each form of abuse presents unique challenges and harms the physical, emotional, and financial well-being of older adults. By increasing awareness, promoting education, and fostering a culture of respect and protection, we can work towards preventing and addressing elder abuse. It is our collective responsibility to ensure the safety, dignity, and well-being of our elderly loved ones.

Statistics and Prevalence of Elder Abuse

Elder abuse is a pervasive problem that affects a significant number of older adults worldwide. However, due to its often hidden and underreported nature, obtaining accurate statistics on elder abuse can be challenging. In this section, we will explore the available data and delve into the prevalence of elder abuse, shedding light on the magnitude of the issue.

The Challenges of Gathering Data

One of the main obstacles in capturing accurate statistics on elder abuse is the reluctance of victims to report the abuse. Many older adults fear retaliation, feel ashamed or embarrassed, or depend on their abusers for care or support. Furthermore, cognitive impairments, such as dementia, may hinder their ability to recognize or communicate the abuse. As a result, the actual prevalence of elder abuse is believed to be much higher than reported figures suggest.

Global Estimates

Although reliable global data on elder abuse is limited, studies and surveys conducted in various countries provide valuable insights into its prevalence. According to the World Health Organization (WHO), around 1 in 6 older adults globally experiences some form of abuse. This estimate, based on available data, suggests that approximately 141 million older adults are affected by elder abuse worldwide.

Physical Abuse

Physical abuse is one of the most visible forms of elder abuse, making it relatively easier to track and document. Studies indicate that physical abuse affects a significant number of older adults. According to the National Center on Elder Abuse (NCEA) in the United States, around 10% of older adults have experienced physical abuse, often resulting in injuries such as bruises, fractures, or internal trauma.

Emotional and Psychological Abuse

Emotional and psychological abuse is challenging to quantify due to its covert nature. However, research and surveys provide insights into its prevalence. Studies suggest that emotional abuse affects approximately 12% of older adults. The abusive behaviors include threats, insults, humiliation, isolation, and manipulation, causing significant psychological distress and undermining the mental well-being of older adults.

Financial Abuse

Financial abuse is a growing concern with serious consequences for older adults. Estimates suggest that between 3% and 5% of older adults experience financial abuse globally. However, this figure is likely an underestimate due to underreporting. Financial abuse can result in significant financial losses, leaving older adults in vulnerable and precarious situations, compromising their ability to meet basic needs and maintain their independence.

Sexual Abuse

Sexual abuse of older adults is a distressing and often unreported form of abuse. Due to social taboos and lack of awareness, reliable statistics on its prevalence are scarce. However, studies indicate that approximately 1-3% of older adults may experience sexual abuse. This form of abuse can have severe physical, emotional, and psychological consequences, leading to trauma and long-lasting effects on the well-being of older adults.

Neglect

Neglect is a prevalent form of elder abuse, particularly in care settings. Studies indicate that neglect affects approximately 14% of older adults. Neglect can manifest as a lack of proper nutrition, inadequate medical care, unsanitary living conditions, or insufficient emotional support. It poses significant risks to the physical and mental well-being of older adults, leading to deteriorating health, injuries, and a compromised quality of life.

Variation in Prevalence

It's important to note that the prevalence of elder abuse varies across countries and cultural contexts. Factors such as societal attitudes towards older adults, access to social support networks, and the quality of elder care services can influence the occurrence and reporting of abuse. Additionally, studies often rely on different methodologies and sample sizes, making direct comparisons between countries challenging.

Elder abuse is a widespread problem affecting millions of older adults worldwide. While accurate statistics on its prevalence are challenging to obtain, available data and research indicate that a significant number of older adults experience various forms of abuse. However, it is crucial to remember that these figures likely underestimate the true scope of the problem due to underreporting and the hidden nature of elder abuse. To address this issue effectively, it is essential to continue raising awareness, improving data collection methodologies, and implementing comprehensive strategies to prevent and respond to elder abuse on a global scale.

Factors Contributing to Elder Abuse

Elder abuse is a complex issue influenced by various factors that contribute to its occurrence. To effectively address and prevent elder abuse, it is crucial to understand these contributing factors and their interplay. In this section, we will explore the underlying causes and circumstances that can lead to elder abuse, shedding light on the complex dynamics involved.

Social Isolation

Social isolation is a significant risk factor for elder abuse. Older adults who lack social connections and support systems are more vulnerable to abuse. Social isolation can result from factors such as the loss of a spouse or friends, geographic distance from family, limited mobility, or limited access to transportation. When older adults are socially isolated, they may become more dependent on others for care and support, increasing their susceptibility to abuse.

Caregiver Stress and Burnout

Caregiver stress and burnout are common factors contributing to elder abuse, particularly within the context of family caregiving. Caring for an older adult can be physically and emotionally demanding, leading to increased levels of stress and exhaustion. Caregivers who are overwhelmed, lack support, or have limited resources may become more prone to abusive behaviors as they struggle to cope with the demands of caregiving. Fatigue, frustration, and feelings of resentment can escalate into abusive actions.

Substance Abuse and Mental Health Issues

Substance abuse and mental health issues, such as addiction, depression, or personality disorders, can contribute to elder abuse. Individuals with substance abuse problems or mental health challenges may be more likely to engage in abusive behaviors towards older adults. These conditions can impair judgment, increase aggression, and compromise the ability to provide appropriate care, putting older adults at risk.

History of Violence or Abuse

Perpetrators of elder abuse may have a history of violence or abuse, either as victims or witnesses. Research suggests that individuals who have experienced violence or abuse earlier in their lives may be more likely to perpetrate abuse in later years. Early exposure to violence can influence the development of maladaptive coping strategies, distorted views of relationships, and a cycle of abuse that continues into older adulthood.

Caregiver Dependency and Power Imbalances

Dependency and power imbalances within caregiving relationships can contribute to elder abuse. Older adults who are reliant on caregivers for their daily needs may fear retaliation or retribution if they disclose abuse. Caregivers who exercise control over the finances, living arrangements, and personal decisions of older adults may exploit their power, leading to financial abuse or other forms of mistreatment.

Ageism and Stereotypes

Ageism, which encompasses negative stereotypes and discrimination against older adults, can contribute to the occurrence of elder abuse. Ageism perpetuates the perception that older adults are vulnerable, frail, or incapable, undermining their autonomy and worth. Such attitudes may contribute to a lack of respect, disregard for their rights, and an increased likelihood of abuse.

Economic and Financial Factors

Financial difficulties, both on the part of the older adult and the caregiver, can contribute to elder abuse. Caregivers experiencing financial strain may resort to exploiting the resources of the older adult for personal gain. Economic dependence on the older adult or financial stressors faced by the older adult can also create an environment conducive to abuse and manipulation.

Cultural and Societal Factors

Cultural and societal factors can influence the occurrence and reporting of elder abuse. Cultural norms, beliefs, and expectations regarding the treatment of older adults may shape the attitudes and behaviors of individuals within a particular community. In some cultures, for example, the hierarchical structure of the family may contribute to a reluctance to report abuse or intervene in family matters.

Elder abuse is a multifaceted issue influenced by various factors. Social isolation, caregiver stress, substance abuse, a history of violence, power imbalances, ageism, economic factors, and cultural influences all contribute to the occurrence of elder abuse. Understanding these contributing factors is vital in developing comprehensive prevention strategies, promoting awareness, and providing appropriate support and resources for older adults and their caregivers. By addressing these underlying causes, we can work towards creating a safer and more respectful environment for older adults, where they can age with dignity and without the fear of abuse.

CHAPTER 2
Recognizing the Signs: Identifying Abuse in Our Loved Ones

In this chapter, we will delve into the crucial task of recognizing the signs of elder abuse. Identifying abuse in our loved ones is of utmost importance to ensure their safety and well-being. By understanding the different forms of abuse and recognizing the indicators, we can take proactive steps to intervene and protect those who may be experiencing mistreatment. This chapter will provide an in-depth exploration of the signs of elder abuse, including physical abuse, emotional abuse, financial abuse, sexual abuse, and neglect.

Physical abuse: bruises, fractures, and signs of neglect

Physical abuse is a distressing form of elder abuse that involves the intentional infliction of pain, injury, or physical harm on an older adult. It leaves visible marks on the body, often in the form of bruises, fractures, or signs of neglect. In this section, we will explore the various aspects of physical abuse, including its indicators, potential consequences, and the importance of recognizing and addressing these signs.

Bruises

Bruising is a common physical indicator of abuse and can occur as a result of physical force or violence directed towards an older adult. Bruises may appear in various stages of healing, ranging from fresh red or purple marks to yellow or greenish discoloration as they fade. Areas commonly prone to bruising due to abuse include the upper arms, thighs, wrists, and neck. Bruises that have unusual shapes or patterns, such as handprints, fingers, or belt marks, may raise suspicions of intentional harm.

It is essential to note that some older adults may have a higher susceptibility to bruising due to age-related factors such as thinner skin, reduced fat tissue, or underlying medical conditions. However, when bruising occurs frequently, in areas inconsistent with accidental injuries, or when explanations are inadequate or conflicting, it is crucial to consider the possibility of physical abuse.

Fractures

Fractures, including broken bones, are severe indicators of physical abuse in older adults. They can result from direct acts of violence such as hitting, pushing, or throwing, or from forced movements that cause excessive strain or impact. Fractures most commonly occur in areas such as the arms, wrists, ribs, hips, or ankles. Older adults with fractures caused by abuse may exhibit significant pain, swelling, deformities, or difficulty moving the affected limb or body part.

It is crucial to differentiate fractures resulting from abuse from those caused by accidental falls or age-related conditions such as osteoporosis. The presence of multiple fractures, fractures in various stages of healing, or fractures inconsistent with the explanations provided raises concerns for intentional harm.

Signs of Neglect

Neglect is a form of physical abuse that involves the failure to provide necessary care, support, or protection to an older adult. Signs of neglect can be both physical and environmental in nature, indicating a lack of adequate care or supervision. Physical indicators may include untreated medical conditions, poor personal hygiene, dehydration, malnutrition, or pressure ulcers (bedsores). The older adult may exhibit signs of weight loss, weakness, fatigue, or general decline in health.

Environmental indicators of neglect may include unsafe living conditions, such as a lack of heating or cooling, inadequate lighting, unclean or cluttered living spaces, or insufficient access to necessary medical equipment or supplies. Neglected older adults may also display signs of social isolation, abandonment, or lack of meaningful social interactions.

Consequences of Physical Abuse

Physical abuse can have severe consequences for the well-being and overall health of older adults. The immediate physical effects may include pain, discomfort, impaired mobility, and increased vulnerability to infections. However, the psychological and emotional impact of physical abuse can be equally detrimental. Older adults who experience physical abuse may develop anxiety, depression, post-traumatic stress disorder (PTSD), or a heightened sense of fear and vulnerability.

Physical abuse can erode trust, disrupt familial or caregiver relationships, and compromise the older adult's sense of safety and autonomy. It can lead to a loss of self-esteem, social withdrawal, or reluctance to seek help or disclose the abuse. The long-term consequences of physical abuse can extend beyond physical injuries, affecting the overall quality of life and well-being of older adults.

Recognizing and Addressing the Signs

Recognizing the signs of physical abuse requires vigilance, observation, and open communication with the older adult. It is essential to develop a trusting relationship that fosters open dialogue and empowers the older adult to share any concerns or experiences of abuse. Caregivers, healthcare professionals, family members, and friends play vital roles in recognizing and addressing the signs of physical abuse.

If physical abuse is suspected, it is crucial to take immediate action to ensure the safety of the older adult. This may involve reporting the abuse to the appropriate authorities, such as adult protective services or law enforcement agencies, documenting the visible signs of abuse through photographs or written descriptions, and providing the necessary support and resources for the older adult to remove themselves from the abusive situation.

Physical abuse, characterized by bruises, fractures, and signs of neglect, is a distressing form of elder abuse that must be recognized and addressed promptly. By being vigilant, observant, and responsive to the signs of physical abuse, we can take the necessary steps to protect the well-being and safety of older adults. It is crucial to foster an environment of trust and open communication, where older adults feel empowered to disclose any abuse they may be experiencing. Through education, awareness, and collective action, we can work towards preventing and ending physical abuse in the lives of our elderly loved ones.

Emotional abuse: isolation, manipulation, and mental anguish

Emotional abuse is a destructive form of elder abuse that inflicts psychological pain, distress, and anguish on older adults. It is characterized by behaviors such as isolation, manipulation, and the deliberate infliction of mental anguish. In this section, we will explore the various aspects of emotional abuse, including its indicators, impact on older adults, and the importance of recognizing and addressing these signs.

Isolation

Isolation is a powerful tactic used in emotional abuse to control and manipulate older adults. Perpetrators may intentionally isolate the older adult from social interactions, friendships, and family relationships. They may limit or restrict contact with others, discourage visits or communication, or create an atmosphere of fear and dependency that prevents the older adult from seeking support or maintaining independent connections.

Indicators of isolation may include the older adult becoming withdrawn, exhibiting signs of loneliness or depression, or expressing feelings of being trapped or powerless. They may have limited opportunities for social engagement, lack meaningful social interactions, or experience a loss of previously enjoyed activities and relationships. The absence of visitors or support systems may also raise concerns about potential emotional abuse.

Manipulation

Manipulation is a key component of emotional abuse, involving tactics aimed at exerting control over the older adult's thoughts, emotions, or actions. Perpetrators may employ techniques such as gaslighting (denying or distorting reality), constant criticism, guilt-tripping, or playing mind games to confuse or undermine the older adult's sense of self-worth, perception of reality, or decision-making abilities.

Signs of manipulation may include the older adult expressing self-doubt, feeling constantly on edge, or exhibiting significant changes in behavior or personality. They may appear hesitant to voice their opinions or make decisions, fearing the consequences of going against the wishes of the abuser. Manipulation can lead to a loss of confidence, diminished self-esteem, and an erosion of the older adult's autonomy and independence.

Mental Anguish

Emotional abuse inflicts significant mental anguish on older adults, causing severe emotional distress and undermining their overall well-being. Perpetrators may engage in relentless criticism, humiliation, or threats to induce fear, anxiety, or emotional pain in the older adult. Verbal or non-verbal aggression, insults, or constant belittling can lead to long-lasting emotional trauma.

Signs of mental anguish may include the older adult displaying signs of depression, anxiety, or post-traumatic stress disorder (PTSD). They may exhibit symptoms such as tearfulness, mood swings, withdrawal from activities or relationships, sleep disturbances, or loss of interest in previously enjoyed hobbies. Mental anguish can also manifest as physical symptoms, including headaches, stomachaches, or exacerbation of pre-existing medical conditions.

Impact on Older Adults

Emotional abuse has profound and long-lasting effects on the well-being and quality of life of older adults. The constant exposure to negative and manipulative behaviors can lead to a decline in mental health, contributing to the development or worsening of mental illnesses such as depression and anxiety disorders. Emotional abuse can also exacerbate existing physical health conditions, as stress and distress can negatively impact the immune system and overall physical well-being.

Older adults who experience emotional abuse may lose confidence in their abilities, become socially isolated, and experience a loss of trust in others. They may develop a heightened sense of fear, feeling trapped in the abusive relationship or environment. Emotional abuse can erode the older adult's self-esteem, self-worth, and sense of identity, resulting in a diminished quality of life and a reluctance to seek help or disclose the abuse.

Recognizing and Addressing the Signs

Recognizing the signs of emotional abuse requires attentiveness, empathy, and open communication with the older adult. Building a trusting relationship and creating a safe environment where the older adult feels empowered to express their emotions and concerns is crucial. Key steps in recognizing and addressing emotional abuse include:

Paying attention to changes in the older adult's behavior, mood, or interactions with others.

- Observing the dynamics between the older adult and their caregivers, family members, or other individuals in their environment.
- Providing opportunities for the older adult to engage in social activities, connect with support networks, and maintain relationships outside the abusive environment.
- Encouraging the older adult to express their feelings, concerns, and experiences without judgment or fear of repercussions.
- Seeking professional help, such as counseling or therapy, to support the emotional well-being of the older adult and address the effects of emotional abuse.

Emotional abuse, characterized by isolation, manipulation, and mental anguish, is a distressing form of elder abuse that has significant impacts on the well-being of older adults. Recognizing the signs of emotional abuse is crucial to protect the emotional and mental health of older adults and to intervene in abusive situations promptly. By fostering open communication, creating supportive environments, and taking proactive steps to address emotional abuse, we can promote the safety, dignity, and well-being of our elderly loved ones.

Financial abuse: exploitation, scams, and undue influence

Financial abuse is a devastating form of elder abuse that involves the unauthorized or improper use of an elderly person's funds, assets, or property. It encompasses various exploitative behaviors, scams, and undue influence. In this section, we will explore the different aspects of financial abuse, including its indicators, impact on older adults, and the importance of recognizing and addressing these signs.

Exploitation

Exploitation is a common form of financial abuse, whereby perpetrators take advantage of an older adult's vulnerability, trust, or dependency for personal gain. Exploitation can occur in various ways, such as

Misuse of Funds

Perpetrators may gain unauthorized access to the older adult's financial resources, including bank accounts, credit cards, or pensions. They may withdraw money without consent, use the funds for personal expenses, or manipulate financial transactions for their own benefit.

Theft or Fraud

Perpetrators may steal cash, valuables, or important documents from the older adult's home or personal belongings. They may also engage in fraudulent activities, such as forging signatures, coercing the older adult into signing over assets, or altering legal documents to gain control over financial resources.

Coercion or Deception

Perpetrators may manipulate the older adult through deceptive tactics or coercion to obtain money or assets. They may create false emergencies, fabricate financial needs, or use emotional manipulation to extract funds or property from the older adult.

Scams

Scams targeting older adults are prevalent forms of financial abuse. Perpetrators use various techniques to deceive older adults into providing personal information, access to bank accounts, or making financial transactions under false pretenses. Common scams include:

Grandparent Scam

Perpetrators pretend to be a grandchild or someone close to the older adult, claiming to be in a dire situation and in need of immediate financial assistance.

Lottery or Sweepstakes Scam

Perpetrators inform the older adult that they have won a lottery or sweepstakes but must pay a fee or provide personal information to claim the prize, resulting in financial loss.

Tech Support Scam

Perpetrators pose as technical support personnel, convincing the older adult that their computer or device has a problem. They gain remote access to the device, stealing personal information or installing malware.

Romance Scam

Perpetrators establish fake online relationships with older adults, building emotional connections and then exploiting them financially by requesting money for various reasons.

Undue Influence

Undue influence refers to the manipulation or coercion exerted by a person in a position of power or trust over the older adult to gain control over their financial decisions. Perpetrators may use their relationship with the older adult, such as a family member, caregiver, or trusted advisor, to exert influence and exploit their vulnerabilities. They may isolate the older adult, limit their access to others, and employ psychological tactics to sway their financial choices.

Impact on Older Adults

Financial abuse has severe consequences for the well-being and security of older adults. The loss of financial resources can result in financial instability, compromising the ability to meet basic needs such as housing, healthcare, and daily expenses. The psychological impact of financial abuse can include feelings of betrayal, shame, embarrassment, and a loss of trust in others.

Financial abuse can also have cascading effects, leading to increased dependency on others, social isolation, and compromised decision-making capacity. Older adults who experience financial abuse may suffer from anxiety, depression, or a sense of powerlessness. The resulting financial distress can exacerbate existing health conditions and diminish their overall quality of life.

Recognizing and Addressing the Signs

Recognizing the signs of financial abuse requires attentiveness, education, and proactive measures. Key steps in recognizing and addressing financial abuse include

Monitoring Financial Activity

Keep an eye on the older adult's financial statements, bank accounts, and transactions for any unusual or unauthorized activities. Look for unexplained withdrawals, sudden changes in spending patterns, or missing funds.

Being Aware of Common Scams

Stay informed about prevalent scams targeting older adults and educate the older adult about these scams to raise their awareness and prevent falling victim to them.

Establishing a Supportive Environment

Create an environment where the older adult feels comfortable discussing their financial matters and concerns. Encourage open communication and foster a trusting relationship to address any signs of financial abuse promptly.

Seeking Professional Assistance

If financial abuse is suspected, consult with legal professionals, financial advisors, or adult protective services to report the abuse, gather evidence, and explore protective measures to safeguard the older adult's financial resources.

Financial abuse, characterized by exploitation, scams, and undue influence, is a grave form of elder abuse that threatens the financial security and well-being of older adults. Recognizing the signs of financial abuse is essential to protect older adults from financial exploitation and to take appropriate actions to address the abuse. By raising awareness, establishing supportive environments, and seeking professional assistance, we can work towards preventing and combatting financial abuse, ensuring the financial stability and dignity of our elderly loved ones.

Sexual abuse: consent, boundaries, and dignity

Sexual abuse is a deeply distressing and violating form of elder abuse that involves any non-consensual sexual contact, coercion, or inappropriate behavior directed towards an older adult. It undermines their autonomy, dignity, and right to live free from harm. In this section, we will explore the various aspects of sexual abuse, including its indicators, impact on older adults, and the importance of recognizing and addressing these signs.

Consent

Consent lies at the heart of any healthy sexual relationship. It is the explicit, voluntary, and ongoing agreement between all parties involved to engage in sexual activity. In the context of elder abuse, older adults may experience sexual abuse when their consent is disregarded or manipulated. Perpetrators may engage in sexual acts without the older adult's informed and enthusiastic consent, exploit their vulnerabilities, or use their position of power or authority to coerce them into unwanted sexual activities.

Understanding and respecting the concept of consent is crucial in preventing and addressing sexual abuse against older adults. Consent should be affirmative, freely given, and obtained without any form of coercion or manipulation.

Boundaries

Maintaining personal boundaries is fundamental to ensuring the safety and well-being of older adults. Sexual abuse violates these boundaries by intruding upon an individual's physical and emotional space. Perpetrators may disregard or trespass these boundaries, engaging in sexual acts without the older adult's explicit consent or against their expressed wishes.

Indicators of boundary violations may include the older adult displaying signs of discomfort, distress, or withdrawal in the presence of specific individuals. They may exhibit changes in behavior, such as increased anxiety, fearfulness, or aversion to physical contact. Paying attention to the older adult's reactions and respecting their boundaries is crucial in preventing and addressing sexual abuse.

Dignity

Sexual abuse strips older adults of their dignity, respect, and inherent worth. It undermines their sense of self and infringes upon their fundamental rights. Older adults who experience sexual abuse may feel a profound loss of dignity, shame, and a reluctance to seek help or disclose the abuse due to feelings of guilt or embarrassment.

Recognizing and affirming the dignity of older adults is vital in preventing and addressing sexual abuse. Creating an environment that respects their autonomy, promotes open communication, and fosters a culture of consent and respect is crucial in ensuring their well-being and preserving their dignity.

Impact on Older Adults

Sexual abuse has devastating consequences for the mental, emotional, and physical well-being of older adults. The trauma resulting from sexual abuse can have long-lasting effects, leading to a range of psychological and emotional challenges. Older adults who experience sexual abuse may suffer from symptoms of post-traumatic stress disorder (PTSD), depression, anxiety, or an increased risk of suicide.

Physical consequences of sexual abuse may include genital or anal injuries, sexually transmitted infections (STIs), or other physical trauma. The older adult may exhibit changes in their sexual behavior, such as a loss of interest in sexual activities, fear or aversion to intimacy, or unexplained pain or discomfort in the genital area.

Recognizing and Addressing the Signs

Recognizing the signs of sexual abuse requires sensitivity, empathy, and a commitment to creating a safe environment for disclosure. Key steps in recognizing and addressing sexual abuse include:

Encouraging open communication

Foster an environment where the older adult feels safe and comfortable discussing matters of a sensitive nature. Encourage open dialogue, active listening, and non-judgmental support.

Observing behavioral changes

Pay attention to any changes in the older adult's behavior, mood, or social interactions. Look for signs of withdrawal, fear, anxiety, or discomfort in the presence of specific individuals.

Trusting the older adult's instincts

Respect the older adult's perceptions and feelings. Validate their experiences and reassure them that they are not at fault for the abuse.

Seeking professional help

Consult with healthcare professionals, therapists, or social workers experienced in elder abuse to provide appropriate support, guidance, and intervention. They can help navigate legal processes, ensure medical care, and provide counseling to address the trauma associated with sexual abuse.

Sexual abuse, characterized by non-consensual sexual contact, boundary violations, and the erosion of dignity, is a deeply traumatic form of elder abuse. Recognizing and addressing the signs of sexual abuse requires creating safe spaces for open communication, promoting consent and respect, and providing the necessary support and resources for older adults who have experienced such abuse. By fostering a culture that upholds the rights, dignity, and autonomy of older adults, we can work towards preventing sexual abuse and ensuring the well-being and safety of our elderly loved ones.

CHAPTER 3
The Profiles of Abusers: Unmasking the Perpetrators

In this chapter, we will delve into the profiles of abusers, seeking to unmask the individuals who perpetrate elder abuse. Understanding the characteristics, motives, and dynamics of abusers is essential in identifying and addressing the root causes of abuse. By shedding light on the profiles of abusers, we can work towards prevention, intervention, and the protection of our elderly loved ones.

Who perpetrates elder abuse?

Elder abuse can be perpetrated by various individuals and groups, each with their own motivations, dynamics, and characteristics. Understanding who perpetrates elder abuse is essential in recognizing and addressing this pervasive issue. In this section, we will explore in detail the different perpetrators of elder abuse, shedding light on their profiles and the factors that contribute to their actions.

Family Members and Caregivers

Family members and caregivers, who are entrusted with the care and support of older adults, can sometimes become perpetrators of elder abuse. This category includes adult children, spouses, partners, other relatives, or individuals providing caregiving services. While the majority of family caregivers provide loving and compassionate care, a subset may exhibit abusive behaviors due to various factors:

Caregiver Stress and Burnout

Providing care for an older adult can be physically, emotionally, and financially demanding. Caregivers may experience high levels of stress, exhaustion, and feelings of burnout, which can lead to abusive behaviors as they struggle to cope with their responsibilities.

Dependency and Power Imbalances

When older adults rely on caregivers for their daily needs, power imbalances can arise. Caregivers may exploit this dependency, asserting control over the older adult's life and resources. This can lead to abusive behaviors and a violation of the older adult's rights and dignity.

History of Family Dysfunction

In some cases, a history of family dysfunction, unresolved conflicts, or strained relationships can contribute to abusive dynamics within caregiving relationships. Long-standing patterns of violence or dysfunctional behaviors may manifest as elder abuse.

Professional Caregivers

Professional caregivers, such as home healthcare workers, nursing home staff, or paid caregivers, also play a role in elder abuse. While the vast majority of professional caregivers provide quality care, a small minority may engage in abusive behaviors due to various factors:

Lack of Training and Supervision

Insufficient training, supervision, or oversight in the caregiving profession can contribute to abusive behaviors. Inadequate knowledge, skills, or resources can result in substandard care or mistreatment of older adults.

Low Pay and Poor Working Conditions

Caregivers who face low wages, long working hours, or stressful work environments may experience job dissatisfaction, frustration, and burnout. These factors can increase the likelihood of abusive behaviors.

Lack of Empathy and Compassion

Some individuals may enter the caregiving profession without possessing the necessary empathy and compassion required to provide quality care. This lack of empathy can contribute to abusive behaviors towards older adults.

Opportunistic Abusers

Opportunistic abusers are individuals who exploit the vulnerabilities of older adults for personal gain. They may not have pre-existing relationships with the older adult but take advantage of opportunities to perpetrate abuse. Characteristics of opportunistic abusers include:

Manipulation and Deception

Opportunistic abusers are skilled at manipulating and deceiving older adults to gain their trust and exploit their vulnerabilities. They may employ tactics such as charm, flattery, false promises, or threats to perpetrate abuse.

Financial Motives

Financial gain is a primary motivation for many opportunistic abusers. They may seek to exploit the older adult's financial resources through scams, fraud, theft, or coercive tactics.

Lack of Empathy and Moral Boundaries

Opportunistic abusers often lack empathy and have few moral qualms about taking advantage of vulnerable individuals. They prioritize their own self-interests above the well-being of the older adult.

Institutional Abusers

Institutional abusers encompass organizations or systems that perpetrate abuse against older adults. This category includes nursing homes, assisted living facilities, hospitals, or other care institutions. Factors contributing to institutional abuse may include

Inadequate Staffing and Training

Insufficient staffing levels and inadequate training of personnel can contribute to the occurrence of abuse within institutional settings. High workload, lack of resources, and limited supervision can foster an environment conducive to abuse.

Neglectful Practices

Institutional abuse may occur through neglectful practices, such as withholding necessary care, failing to address medical needs promptly, or providing substandard living conditions.

Lack of Oversight and Accountability

In some instances, institutional abusers may exploit the lack of effective oversight and accountability mechanisms within the care system. This can enable the perpetuation of abusive behaviors.

Elder abuse can be perpetrated by family members, caregivers, professional caregivers, opportunistic abusers, and institutional systems. Understanding the profiles of abusers and the factors contributing to their actions is crucial in recognizing and addressing elder abuse. By raising awareness, providing support, implementing appropriate training, and promoting accountability within caregiving relationships and institutions, we can work towards preventing and mitigating elder abuse, ensuring the safety, dignity, and well-being of our elderly loved ones.

Recognizing the red flags in caregivers, family members, and institutions

Recognizing the red flags in caregivers, family members, and institutions is crucial in identifying potential cases of elder abuse. By being vigilant and aware of certain indicators, we can take proactive steps to address and prevent abuse. In this section, we will explore in detail the red flags associated with caregivers, family members, and institutions, along with their explanations.

Red Flags in Caregivers: Sudden Changes in Behavior

If a caregiver exhibits abrupt changes in behavior, such as increased irritability, impatience, or aggression, it may be a sign of potential abuse. Mood swings or unexplained emotional volatility should not be ignored.

Lack of Empathy and Compassion

Caregivers who consistently display a lack of empathy, compassion, or concern for the older adult's well-being may indicate a higher risk of abusive behavior. They may exhibit indifference towards the older adult's needs or dismiss their feelings and preferences.

Isolation of the Older Adult

Caregivers who actively isolate the older adult from friends, family members, or social activities may be exerting control and perpetrating abuse. Limiting access to support networks can prevent the older adult from disclosing abuse or seeking help.

Financial Exploitation

Signs of financial exploitation by caregivers include unexplained withdrawals from the older adult's accounts, unauthorized use of their funds, or sudden changes in financial circumstances. Caregivers who frequently request or demand money from the older adult may be exploiting their financial resources.

Neglecting Basic Care Needs

If a caregiver consistently neglects the older adult's basic care needs, such as personal hygiene, nutrition, or medication management, it may indicate neglect or abusive behavior. Unattended health conditions, poor living conditions, or untreated medical issues are red flags that require attention.

Red Flags in Family Members: Frequent Arguments or Tension

Family environment characterized by frequent arguments, tension, or hostility may be indicative of a higher risk of elder abuse. Unresolved conflicts or ongoing power struggles can contribute to abusive dynamics within the family.

Control and Isolation

Family members who exert excessive control over the older adult's daily activities, restrict their independence, or isolate them from social connections may be engaging in abusive behavior. This control can manifest through restrictions on communication, limitations on personal choices, or attempts to manipulate the older adult's decisions.

History of Violence or Abuse

If there is a documented history of violence, abuse, or dysfunctional family dynamics within the family, it raises concerns for potential elder abuse. Previous instances of abuse or neglect towards children or other family members may serve as red flags for elder abuse.

Financial Mismanagement

Family members who misuse or exploit the older adult's financial resources, fail to provide necessary financial support, or exhibit control over their financial decisions may be engaging in financial abuse. Unexplained changes in the older adult's financial circumstances or sudden depletion of their assets are warning signs.

Red Flags in Institutions: Inadequate Staffing Levels

Institutions that consistently operate with insufficient staffing levels may compromise the quality of care provided to older adults. Overworked and overwhelmed staff may be more likely to engage in neglectful or abusive behaviors.

Poor Staff-Resident Interactions

Observe the interactions between staff and residents within an institution. Red flags include disrespectful or dismissive behavior towards older adults, frequent yelling or harsh tones, or instances of belittlement or humiliation.

Unsanitary or Unsafe Conditions

Institutions that fail to maintain clean, hygienic, and safe living environments may indicate neglectful or abusive practices. Examples include inadequate food hygiene, unclean living spaces, inadequate access to proper sanitation facilities, or lack of appropriate safety measures.

Lack of Documentation or Transparency

Institutions that exhibit a lack of proper documentation, transparency, or accountability in their operations may raise concerns. Difficulty obtaining information about the older adult's care, treatment, or finances can be a red flag for potential abuse or neglect.

Recognizing the red flags in caregivers, family members, and institutions is essential in identifying potential cases of elder abuse. By remaining vigilant and attentive to behavioral changes, lack of empathy, financial irregularities, neglectful practices, and other indicators, we can take proactive steps to address and prevent abuse. It is crucial to create awareness, promote open communication, and establish systems for reporting and addressing concerns to ensure the safety, well-being, and dignity of our elderly loved ones.

Understanding the psychology of abusers

Understanding the psychology of abusers is a complex endeavor that requires examining the underlying factors, motivations, and dynamics that contribute to their abusive behaviors. By exploring the psychology of abusers, we can gain insights into the patterns of thinking, emotions, and behaviors that drive their actions. In this section, we will delve into the psychology of abusers, shedding light on common factors and psychological dynamics associated with their behavior.

Power and Control

One prominent psychological aspect of abusers is the desire for power and control. Abusers seek to establish dominance over their victims, using various tactics to assert control and maintain a position of power. This desire for control may stem from feelings of inadequacy, a need to compensate for their own vulnerabilities, or a desire to exert authority over others. By controlling their victims, abusers derive a sense of power and satisfaction, which reinforces their abusive behaviors.

Low Empathy and Lack of Remorse

Abusers often display a lack of empathy towards their victims, making it easier for them to engage in abusive behaviors without experiencing guilt or remorse. This lack of empathy allows them to disregard the feelings, well-being, and rights of the older adult. Abusers may have difficulty understanding or connecting with the emotions and perspectives of their victims, further enabling their abusive actions.

Manipulation and Deception

Abusers are adept at manipulating and deceiving their victims to achieve their desired outcomes. They may employ tactics such as gaslighting (distorting or denying reality), emotional manipulation, or playing mind games to confuse, control, and undermine the older adult's sense of self-worth, perception of reality, or decision-making abilities. By manipulating their victims, abusers maintain a position of power and control over them.

Cycle of Violence

Many abusers exhibit a pattern of abusive behavior known as the cycle of violence. This cycle typically consists of three stages: tension building, the acute abusive incident, and the honeymoon phase. During the tension-building stage, minor conflicts, arguments, or frustrations occur, leading to increased tension and anxiety. The acute abusive incident is characterized by an explosive outburst of abuse, which may be physical, emotional, or sexual in nature. Following the abusive incident, the abuser often enters the honeymoon phase, characterized by apologies, promises, and displays of affection, aimed at reconciling and manipulating the victim into staying in the abusive relationship. This cycle repeats, with the tension-building stage gradually escalating over time.

Personal and Psychological Factors

Abusers may have personal and psychological factors that contribute to their abusive behaviors. These factors can vary widely among individuals, but some common characteristics include

History of Abuse

Many abusers have experienced abuse themselves, either as children or in past relationships. This history of abuse can perpetuate a cycle of violence, as they may model their behavior on what they have witnessed or experienced.

Low Self-Esteem

Abusers may have low self-esteem, leading them to seek power and control over others as a means of boosting their own sense of self-worth. Abusing others allows them to temporarily alleviate their own feelings of inadequacy and gain a false sense of superiority.

Personality Disorders

Some abusers may exhibit traits associated with personality disorders, such as narcissistic personality disorder or antisocial personality disorder. These disorders can contribute to a lack of empathy, an inflated sense of self-importance, and a disregard for the rights and well-being of others.

Social and Cultural Factors

Social and cultural factors can also influence the psychology of abusers. Norms and beliefs that perpetuate gender inequality, acceptance of violence, or the idea of entitlement can contribute to the development of abusive behaviors. Societal attitudes that condone or minimize the severity of elder abuse may further enable abusers to justify their actions and continue their abusive behaviors.

Understanding the psychology of abusers is a complex task, as it involves examining the underlying factors, motivations, and dynamics that contribute to their abusive behaviors. Abusers seek power and control over their victims, display a lack of empathy, and engage in manipulation and deception to maintain their dominance. Factors such as a history of abuse, low self-esteem, personality disorders, and societal influences play a role in shaping the psychology of abusers. By gaining insights into the psychology of abusers, we can work towards prevention, intervention, and the establishment of support systems that promote the safety, well-being, and dignity of older adults.

CHAPTER 4
Unveiling the Dark Corners: Exploring Settings Prone to Abuse

In this chapter, we will delve into the settings that are prone to elder abuse, shedding light on the dark corners where abuse can occur. By understanding the characteristics and dynamics of these settings, we can take proactive steps to identify and address the risk factors that contribute to elder abuse. This exploration will help us create safer environments for our elderly loved ones.

Home Settings

Home settings, where older adults often receive care from family members or hired caregivers, can be vulnerable to elder abuse. Several factors contribute to the risk of abuse in home settings:

Isolation

Older adults who live in isolation or have limited social interactions may be at higher risk of abuse. The absence of regular interactions with others makes it easier for abusers to exert control and conceal their abusive behaviors.

Dependency

Older adults who depend on others for their daily care needs may be more susceptible to abuse. This dependency creates power imbalances and can lead to the exploitation of the older adult's vulnerability.

Caregiver Stress

Caregivers who provide care in the home setting may experience high levels of stress, which can increase the likelihood of abusive behaviors. Factors such as lack of support, inadequate respite care, and overwhelming caregiving responsibilities contribute to caregiver stress.

Lack of Oversight

Unlike institutional settings, home settings often lack formal oversight or monitoring. This lack of oversight makes it easier for abuse to go unnoticed or unreported.

Institutional Settings

Institutional settings, including nursing homes, assisted living facilities, and hospitals, also pose risks for elder abuse. While the majority of institutions provide quality care, certain factors can contribute to abuse within these settings:

Inadequate Staffing

Insufficient staffing levels and high staff turnover can result in a strained caregiving environment. Understaffing increases the workload on individual caregivers, compromising the quality of care and creating an environment prone to neglect and abuse.

Lack of Training and Supervision

Inadequate training and supervision of staff members can contribute to abusive behaviors. Staff who are ill-prepared to handle the complex needs of older adults or who lack knowledge of elder abuse prevention may be more likely to engage in abusive practices.

Staff Burnout and Job Dissatisfaction

Healthcare professionals who experience burnout, job dissatisfaction, or compassion fatigue may be more prone to exhibiting abusive behaviors. Overworked and emotionally drained staff may not provide the necessary care and attention to older adults, leading to neglect or mistreatment.

Culture of Acceptance

Some institutional settings may have a culture that tolerates or overlooks abusive behaviors. A lack of accountability, failure to address complaints, or a dismissive attitude towards elder abuse concerns can contribute to an environment where abuse thrives.

Community and Social Settings

Community and social settings can also harbor risks for elder abuse. These settings include social groups, day centers, or places where older adults gather for recreational or social activities. Factors that contribute to the risk of abuse in community settings include:

Lack of Awareness and Education

Insufficient knowledge and awareness about elder abuse within the community can make it easier for abuse to go unnoticed or unrecognized. Older adults and community members may not be familiar with the signs of abuse or know how to respond when abuse is suspected.

Exploitation by Scammers

Older adults can be targeted by scammers who take advantage of their trust, vulnerability, or financial resources. Scams targeting older adults, such as fraudulent investment schemes or fake charities, can result in financial abuse and exploitation.

Ageism and Stereotyping

Ageism, prejudice, and stereotypes about older adults can contribute to the perpetuation of abuse. Negative attitudes towards older adults can lead to a disregard for their well-being, resulting in neglect or mistreatment.

Lack of Supportive Services

Inadequate availability of support services, such as counseling, legal aid, or social assistance, within the community can hinder the identification and intervention of elder abuse cases.

Certain settings are more prone to elder abuse due to various risk factors and dynamics. Home settings, institutional settings, and community/social settings each present unique challenges in addressing and preventing elder abuse. By recognizing the characteristics and vulnerabilities of these settings, we can implement targeted interventions, such as increased oversight, caregiver support programs, education and training initiatives, and enhanced community resources. By shining a light on the dark corners where abuse can occur, we can work towards creating safer environments for older adults, fostering a society that values and protects the well-being and dignity of our elderly loved ones.

Nursing homes and assisted living facilities

Nursing homes and assisted living facilities play a critical role in providing care and support for older adults who require assistance with daily activities or have specific medical needs. While the majority of these facilities strive to provide quality care, there have been instances of elder abuse occurring within these settings. In this section, we will explore nursing homes and assisted living facilities in detail, shedding light on the factors, challenges, and measures that can contribute to creating safe and nurturing environments for older adults.

Nursing Homes

Nursing homes, also known as skilled nursing facilities, cater to older adults with complex medical needs or those requiring round-the-clock care. Understanding the dynamics and challenges within nursing homes is essential in preventing and addressing elder abuse. Key aspects to consider include:

Medical Care and Oversight

Nursing homes provide medical care, supervision, and assistance with activities of daily living for older adults. These facilities employ licensed healthcare professionals, including nurses and doctors, who are responsible for managing the medical needs of residents. However, inadequate staffing levels, high turnover rates, or insufficient training can compromise the quality of care and contribute to the risk of abuse.

Resident-to-Staff Ratio

Adequate staffing is crucial to ensuring the well-being and safety of nursing home residents. An optimal resident-to-staff ratio allows caregivers to provide personalized attention, monitor residents' health, and respond promptly to their needs. Insufficient staffing levels can lead to neglect, inadequate supervision, and increased stress levels among caregivers, which may result in abusive behaviors.

Staff Training and Education

Comprehensive and ongoing training is essential for nursing home staff to effectively address the specific needs of older adults, including identifying and preventing elder abuse. Training should cover topics such as recognizing signs of abuse, communication techniques, person-centered care, and ethical responsibilities. Investing in staff training can foster a culture of compassion, empathy, and professional accountability.

Regulatory Oversight

Regulatory bodies play a vital role in monitoring and ensuring the quality of care in nursing homes. Government agencies, such as the Centers for Medicare and Medicaid Services (CMS), conduct regular inspections, enforce standards, and investigate complaints related to elder abuse and neglect. Strong regulatory oversight and enforcement are crucial for maintaining accountability and promoting safe environments for residents.

Assisted Living Facilities

Assisted living facilities provide a middle ground between independent living and nursing home care. They offer supportive services and assistance with daily activities, such as bathing, dressing, and medication management, while promoting residents' independence and autonomy. Understanding the unique characteristics and challenges of assisted living facilities is essential in addressing elder abuse. Key aspects include:

Person-Centered Care

Assisted living facilities prioritize person-centered care, focusing on meeting individual needs, preferences, and promoting residents' autonomy. This approach encourages residents' active participation in decision-making, fostering a sense of dignity, choice, and control over their lives.

Resident Rights and Freedom

Assisted living facilities should uphold residents' rights and protect their freedom. This includes respecting their privacy, maintaining confidentiality, allowing residents to make choices about their daily routines, and ensuring their safety and security.

Staff Training and Competency

Assisted living facility staff should receive training that equips them with the skills and knowledge necessary to support residents' needs while preventing abuse. Training should cover topics such as recognizing signs of abuse, communication skills, person-centered care, and ethical responsibilities. Ongoing education and professional development are essential to keep staff updated on best practices and standards of care.

Supportive Environment

Assisted living facilities should foster a supportive and inclusive environment that promotes social engagement, opportunities for meaningful activities, and resident interaction. By providing a sense of community, facilities can help prevent isolation, enhance well-being, and reduce the risk of abuse.

Prevention and Intervention Measures

To create safe and nurturing environments within nursing homes and assisted living facilities, several measures can be implemented

Enhanced Staff Screening

Thorough background checks, reference verifications, and pre-employment screenings can help identify potential red flags in prospective staff members. This includes screening for previous incidents of abuse or misconduct.

Rigorous Staff Training

Comprehensive training programs should be implemented to educate staff members about the signs of abuse, resident rights, ethical responsibilities, communication skills, and best practices for person-centered care. Ongoing training and refresher courses are essential to reinforce knowledge and promote continuous improvement.

Encouraging Reporting and Whistleblower Protection

Establishing clear reporting mechanisms, confidential hotlines, and whistleblower protection policies can encourage staff, residents, and family members to report any suspected cases of abuse without fear of retaliation. Anonymous reporting options can also be made available.

Quality Assurance and Regular Inspections

Regular inspections, conducted by regulatory bodies, help ensure compliance with quality standards and identify areas requiring improvement. These inspections should assess staffing levels, staff competency, resident well-being, and adherence to abuse prevention protocols.

Resident and Family Involvement

Encouraging resident and family involvement in care planning, decision-making, and facility governance fosters transparency, trust, and accountability. Regular communication channels and family councils can provide opportunities for feedback, discussion, and addressing concerns related to elder abuse.

Nursing homes and assisted living facilities have a crucial role in providing care and support to older adults. By understanding the dynamics, challenges, and measures associated with these settings, we can work towards creating safe environments that prioritize the well-being, dignity, and rights of older adults. By investing in adequate staffing, comprehensive training, regulatory oversight, and fostering person-centered care, we can reduce the risk of elder abuse and promote the highest quality of care for our elderly loved ones.

Home care agencies and private caregivers

Home care agencies and private caregivers play a significant role in providing care and support to older adults in their own homes. These services enable older adults to age in place while receiving assistance with daily activities and personalized care. While most home care agencies and private caregivers are dedicated professionals committed to the well-being of their clients, it is crucial to understand the dynamics, challenges, and measures associated with these services to prevent elder abuse. In this section, we will explore home care agencies and private caregivers in detail.

Home Care Agencies

Home care agencies employ caregivers who provide services in clients' homes. These agencies often have structured systems and protocols in place to ensure the quality of care and the safety of older adults. Key aspects to consider include:

Caregiver Screening and Training

Home care agencies typically conduct thorough background checks, including criminal records and reference verifications, to ensure the suitability and trustworthiness of their caregivers. They also provide training to their staff members, equipping them with the necessary skills, knowledge, and best practices for providing care to older adults.

Supervision and Support

Home care agencies typically have supervisors or care coordinators who oversee the care provided by caregivers. Regular supervision and support help ensure that caregivers adhere to professional standards, address any concerns, and provide high-quality care. Supervisors also serve as points of contact for clients and their families to raise any issues or questions.

Flexibility and Continuity of Care

Home care agencies offer flexibility in terms of scheduling and the types of services provided. They strive to match clients with caregivers based on the specific needs and preferences of the older adults. Agencies also have contingency plans in place to ensure continuity of care in the event that a caregiver becomes unavailable.

Regulatory Oversight

In many jurisdictions, home care agencies are subject to regulatory oversight to ensure compliance with quality standards, caregiver qualifications, and client safety. Government agencies or licensing bodies may conduct inspections, investigate complaints, and enforce regulations to protect the well-being of older adults.

Private Caregivers

Private caregivers are individuals hired directly by older adults or their families to provide in-home care. While private caregivers offer personalized care tailored to the specific needs of the older adult, additional considerations are necessary to ensure the safety and well-being of both parties. Key aspects include:

Thorough Screening and Reference Checks

When hiring a private caregiver, it is essential to conduct thorough screening, including background checks, interviews, and reference verifications. Engaging professional services to perform these checks can help ensure the caregiver's reliability, trustworthiness, and suitability for the role.

Clear Expectations and Agreements

Establishing clear expectations, job descriptions, and written agreements with the private caregiver is crucial. This includes defining responsibilities, working hours, compensation, and protocols for reporting concerns or addressing issues that may arise during the caregiving relationship.

Ongoing Communication and Monitoring

Regular communication with the private caregiver is essential to ensure the older adult's needs are being met and to address any emerging concerns. Periodic check-ins, meetings, or feedback sessions help maintain open lines of communication and provide an opportunity to assess the quality of care being provided.

Backup and Respite Care

Private caregivers may require time off or become unavailable due to personal reasons. It is important to have backup plans or arrangements in place to ensure continuity of care. Respite care services, which provide temporary relief for family caregivers, can also be valuable to prevent caregiver burnout and maintain the well-being of both the caregiver and the older adult.

Education and Training

Private caregivers should possess the necessary skills and training to provide safe and appropriate care. Encouraging them to participate in educational programs, workshops, or certification courses specific to elder care can enhance their knowledge and competence.

Prevention and Intervention Measures

To prevent elder abuse within home care agencies and with private caregivers, several measures can be implemented:

Client and Family Education

Home care agencies and private caregivers should prioritize client and family education about elder abuse, including recognizing signs of abuse, understanding boundaries, and knowing how to report concerns or seek help. Educational materials, workshops, or informational sessions can be provided to enhance awareness and promote proactive actions.

Monitoring and Feedback Systems

Home care agencies can implement monitoring systems, such as satisfaction surveys or regular check-ins, to gather feedback from clients and their families. These systems help identify any issues, assess the quality of care, and provide opportunities for improvement.

Reporting Mechanisms

Home care agencies and private caregivers should establish clear reporting mechanisms for clients and their families to report any concerns or suspicions of abuse. Confidential hotlines or contact persons can be designated to ensure the privacy and protection of those reporting potential abuse.

Collaboration with Community Resources

Home care agencies and private caregivers can collaborate with community organizations, such as elder abuse helplines, social services, or advocacy groups, to access additional support, resources, and expertise in addressing elder abuse.

Home care agencies and private caregivers play a vital role in supporting older adults to age in place. By understanding the dynamics, challenges, and measures associated with these services, we can promote the well-being, safety, and dignity of older adults receiving care in their homes. Thorough screening, training, supervision, clear communication, and collaboration with community resources are key elements in preventing elder abuse and ensuring high-quality care. Through these efforts, we can create nurturing environments where older adults can receive the support they need while maintaining their independence and dignity.

Family dynamics and intergenerational abuse

Family dynamics and intergenerational abuse are complex topics that require careful examination to understand the factors, patterns, and impacts of abuse within families across generations. By exploring family dynamics and intergenerational abuse, we can gain insights into the underlying causes, dynamics, and consequences of abuse within family units. In this section, we will delve into these topics in detail, shedding light on the complexities and implications they present.

Family Dynamics

Family dynamics refer to the patterns, interactions, and relationships that exist within a family unit. These dynamics play a significant role in shaping individual behaviors, communication styles, and power structures. Several factors influence family dynamics, including:

Power Imbalances

Family dynamics often involve varying levels of power distribution among family members. Power imbalances can arise from factors such as age, gender, socioeconomic status, or cultural norms. When power is disproportionately held by one or a few family members, it can contribute to abusive behaviors.

Communication Patterns

Communication styles within families can impact how conflicts, emotions, and needs are expressed and addressed. Open and healthy communication allows for the sharing of feelings, concerns, and problem-solving, while poor communication or the presence of toxic communication patterns can contribute to misunderstandings, hostility, and abusive dynamics.

Role Expectations

Each family member may be assigned certain roles or responsibilities based on societal or cultural expectations. These roles can influence power dynamics and interactions within the family. When role expectations are rigidly enforced or when individuals are forced into roles that do not align with their capabilities or desires, it can create tension and contribute to abusive behaviors.

Intergenerational Abuse

Intergenerational abuse refers to the perpetuation of abusive behaviors within families across generations. It occurs when patterns of abuse, whether physical, emotional, sexual, or financial, are passed down from one generation to the next. Key aspects to consider in understanding intergenerational abuse include

Learned Behavior

Individuals who have grown up witnessing or experiencing abuse within their families may internalize those behaviors as normal or acceptable. As they become parents or caregivers themselves, they may unintentionally repeat the patterns of abuse they learned in childhood.

Cycle of Violence

The cycle of violence is a pattern commonly observed in intergenerational abuse. It involves three stages: tension building, acute abusive incident, and a period of calm or reconciliation. The cycle repeats over time, with each generation experiencing similar patterns of abuse.

Emotional and Psychological Impact

Intergenerational abuse can have profound emotional and psychological impacts on individuals. Survivors of abuse may carry trauma, unresolved anger, or feelings of powerlessness into adulthood. These unresolved emotions can contribute to abusive behaviors or the perpetuation of abuse in subsequent generations.

Cultural and Societal Factors

Cultural and societal factors can influence intergenerational abuse. Norms that condone or tolerate abusive behaviors, beliefs about power dynamics within families, or stigmatization around seeking help can perpetuate intergenerational abuse.

Breaking the Cycle

Breaking the cycle of intergenerational abuse is crucial to creating healthier family dynamics and promoting the well-being of future generations. Strategies for breaking the cycle include:

Education and Awareness

Providing education and awareness about healthy relationships, parenting skills, and the impact of abuse is vital. This can empower individuals to recognize and challenge abusive patterns and seek help when needed.

Therapy and Counseling

Offering therapy and counseling services to survivors of abuse can support their healing process and help them develop healthier coping mechanisms and relationship skills. Family therapy can also be beneficial in addressing the underlying issues and dynamics that contribute to intergenerational abuse.

Supportive Resources

Accessible and comprehensive support resources, such as helplines, support groups, and community programs, are essential in helping individuals navigate the challenges of intergenerational abuse. These resources can provide emotional support, practical assistance, and guidance for breaking the cycle of abuse.

Parenting Programs

Providing parenting programs that focus on positive parenting techniques, communication skills, and stress management can help individuals develop healthier parenting styles and break the cycle of abuse within their own families.

Family dynamics and intergenerational abuse are complex subjects that require deep exploration and understanding. By recognizing the power dynamics, communication patterns, and role expectations within families, we can gain insights into the factors that contribute to intergenerational abuse. Breaking the cycle of abuse through education, therapy, supportive resources, and parenting programs is crucial for promoting healthy family dynamics and preventing the perpetuation of abusive behaviors across generations. By creating safe, nurturing, and supportive environments, we can support individuals in breaking free from the cycle of abuse and building healthier, more compassionate family relationships.

Chapter 5
Breaking the Silence: Encouraging Reporting and Intervention

In this chapter, we will explore the importance of breaking the silence surrounding elder abuse and creating a culture that encourages reporting and intervention. By understanding the barriers to reporting, promoting awareness, and implementing effective intervention strategies, we can empower individuals to take action and protect older adults from abuse. This chapter will delve into the topic in detail, shedding light on the significance of breaking the silence and promoting a proactive approach to addressing elder abuse.

Barriers to Reporting

Before addressing the strategies to encourage reporting and intervention, it is essential to recognize the barriers that prevent individuals from reporting elder abuse. Some common barriers include:

Fear and Shame

Victims of elder abuse often experience fear and shame, which may prevent them from speaking out or seeking help. They may fear retaliation, loss of support, or further abuse. The stigma associated with being a victim of abuse can also contribute to feelings of shame and reluctance to disclose their experiences.

Dependency and Power Imbalances

Older adults who rely on their abusers for care and support may feel trapped and dependent, making it challenging to report the abuse. Power imbalances within relationships, especially when the abuser is a family member or caregiver, can create a sense of powerlessness and fear of consequences.

Lack of Awareness

Many individuals, including older adults themselves, may lack awareness about the signs and forms of elder abuse. They may not recognize abusive behaviors or may dismiss them as a normal part of aging or family dynamics. Without adequate knowledge, they may not realize that they have the right to report and seek assistance.

Communication and Cognitive Barriers

Some older adults may face communication or cognitive challenges that hinder their ability to report abuse. This could be due to language barriers, cognitive decline, or health conditions that affect their ability to articulate their experiences or seek help.

Promoting Awareness and Education

To encourage reporting and intervention, it is crucial to raise awareness about elder abuse and its consequences. Key strategies include

Public Awareness Campaigns

Launching public awareness campaigns to educate the general population about elder abuse, its signs, and the importance of reporting is crucial. These campaigns can utilize various mediums, including television, radio, social media, and community events, to reach a wide audience and promote understanding.

Targeted Outreach

Implementing targeted outreach programs that specifically focus on reaching older adults, caregivers, and professionals in relevant fields, such as healthcare, social services, and law enforcement, can enhance awareness and knowledge about elder abuse. These programs can provide educational materials, workshops, and training sessions to equip individuals with the tools to recognize and respond to elder abuse.

Community Engagement

Engaging community organizations, faith-based groups, and local agencies in the conversation about elder abuse can help foster supportive networks and resources for reporting and intervention. Collaboration with these entities can result in the development of community-specific strategies and support systems.

Empowering Older Adults

Empowering older adults to assert their rights, speak up, and report abuse is crucial. Providing older adults with information about their rights, avenues for reporting, and access to supportive services empowers them to take action against abuse.

Effective Intervention Strategies

Implementing effective intervention strategies is essential for responding to reported cases of elder abuse and providing appropriate support. Key strategies include

Multidisciplinary Approach

Establishing multidisciplinary teams comprised of professionals from various fields, such as healthcare, social services, law enforcement, legal, and financial sectors, can ensure a comprehensive and coordinated response to reported cases of elder abuse. These teams can collaborate, share information, and develop intervention plans tailored to the specific needs of each case.

Enhanced Reporting Mechanisms

Implementing accessible and confidential reporting mechanisms, such as helplines or online reporting platforms, encourages individuals to come forward with their concerns. These mechanisms should be widely promoted, easily accessible, and designed to accommodate different communication needs, including those of older adults with disabilities or language barriers.

Support Services

Providing a range of support services, including counseling, legal assistance, financial counseling, and emergency shelters, is crucial for addressing the needs of older adults who have experienced abuse. These services should be readily available, culturally sensitive, and specialized to meet the unique challenges faced by older adults.

Legal and Protective Measures

Strengthening legal frameworks and protective measures can act as deterrents to elder abuse and provide avenues for justice. This may include enacting legislation that explicitly criminalizes elder abuse, establishing protective orders, and enhancing penalties for offenders.

Breaking the silence surrounding elder abuse and encouraging reporting and intervention is essential in protecting older adults from abuse. By addressing the barriers to reporting, promoting awareness and education, and implementing effective intervention strategies, we can create a society that prioritizes the safety, well-being, and dignity of older adults. It requires a collective effort from individuals, communities, organizations, and governments to foster a culture where reporting abuse is encouraged, and supportive systems are in place to respond to cases of elder abuse promptly and effectively. By taking action, we can empower older adults, hold abusers accountable, and work towards creating a world free from elder abuse.

Overcoming barriers to reporting

Overcoming barriers to reporting is crucial in addressing and preventing elder abuse. By understanding the barriers that individuals face when reporting abuse and implementing strategies to overcome them, we can create a supportive environment that encourages victims and witnesses to come forward. In this section, we will explore the common barriers to reporting elder abuse and discuss effective ways to overcome them.

Fear and Shame

Fear and shame are significant barriers that prevent individuals from reporting elder abuse. Victims may fear retaliation, further abuse, or the loss of support networks. Feelings of shame and embarrassment can also discourage victims from speaking out about their experiences. Overcoming this barrier requires creating an environment where individuals feel safe and empowered to report abuse. Strategies to address fear and shame include:

Confidential Reporting

Establishing confidential reporting mechanisms, such as helplines, online platforms, or anonymous reporting options, can provide a sense of security for individuals who fear retribution or exposure. Ensuring confidentiality is crucial to encouraging victims and witnesses to come forward.

Empowerment and Support

Providing support services, including counseling, advocacy, and legal assistance, helps empower victims and reduces the sense of isolation and shame. Educating individuals about their rights and available resources can boost their confidence in reporting abuse.

Awareness Campaigns

Public awareness campaigns that emphasize the importance of reporting, highlight success stories of survivors, and challenge the stigma associated with being a victim of abuse can help change societal attitudes and reduce the feelings of shame or embarrassment.

Dependency and Power Imbalances

Dependency on abusers and power imbalances within relationships can create barriers to reporting elder abuse. Older adults may feel trapped or dependent on their abusers for care, finances, or emotional support. Overcoming this barrier requires providing individuals with alternatives and support to break free from abusive situations. Strategies to address dependency and power imbalances include:

Accessible Support Services

Ensuring that a range of support services, such as shelters, counseling, financial assistance, and healthcare, are readily available can provide victims with the resources they need to become independent from their abusers.

Empowering Decision-Making

Empowering older adults to make decisions about their lives, health, and finances can help reduce their dependency on abusers. Providing information, education, and supportive guidance on decision-making and autonomy can empower older adults to assert their rights and seek help when needed.

Encouraging Support Networks

Facilitating connections with supportive family members, friends, and community organizations can help victims build a network of people who can provide assistance and resources. Supportive relationships outside the abusive situation can strengthen individuals' resolve to break free from abuse.

Lack of Awareness

Lack of awareness about the signs and forms of elder abuse can hinder reporting. Many individuals, including older adults themselves, may not recognize abusive behaviors or understand their rights in abusive situations. Overcoming this barrier requires comprehensive education and awareness campaigns. Strategies to address the lack of awareness include:

Educational Programs

Implementing educational programs that raise awareness about elder abuse, its signs, and its consequences is crucial. These programs can be targeted at older adults, caregivers, professionals in relevant fields, and the general public. Providing information about reporting channels and available support services is essential in empowering individuals to take action.

Collaboration with Community Organizations

Partnering with community organizations, senior centers, healthcare providers, and faith-based groups can help disseminate information about elder abuse and promote reporting. These organizations can serve as trusted sources of information and support within the community.

Public Awareness Campaigns

Launching public awareness campaigns through various media channels, including television, radio, social media, and community events, can reach a wide audience and educate the public about the signs of elder abuse and the importance of reporting. These campaigns should emphasize that reporting abuse is a civic responsibility and can save lives.

Communication and Cognitive Barriers

Communication and cognitive challenges faced by older adults can impede their ability to report abuse. Language barriers, cognitive decline, or health conditions may hinder their articulation of their experiences or understanding of the reporting process. Overcoming this barrier requires tailored approaches and support. Strategies to address communication and cognitive barriers include:

Multilingual Support

Providing multilingual helplines, interpreters, and written materials in different languages ensures that language barriers do not prevent individuals from reporting abuse. Culturally sensitive support services should be available to individuals from diverse linguistic backgrounds.

Communication Aids

Offering communication aids, such as picture-based reporting tools, simplified forms, or assistive technologies, can assist older adults with cognitive challenges in expressing their experiences. Training professionals and caregivers to communicate effectively with older adults with cognitive impairments is also essential.

Collaboration with Professionals

Collaborating with healthcare professionals, social workers, and geriatric specialists who have expertise in communicating with older adults can enhance the reporting process. These professionals can employ appropriate techniques to facilitate effective communication and build trust with older adults.

Overcoming barriers to reporting is critical in addressing elder abuse and providing support to victims. By addressing fear and shame, dependency and power imbalances, lack of awareness, and communication and cognitive barriers, we can create an environment that encourages reporting and intervention. Implementing strategies such as confidential reporting mechanisms, awareness campaigns, accessible support services, empowerment, and tailored communication approaches can help individuals overcome these barriers. By breaking the silence and creating a culture that supports reporting, we can take significant strides towards preventing elder abuse and promoting the well-being and safety of older adults.

The importance of bystander intervention

The importance of bystander intervention in addressing elder abuse cannot be overstated. Bystanders, who witness or suspect abusive situations, have a crucial role to play in preventing harm, supporting victims, and promoting a culture that rejects abuse. By understanding the significance of bystander intervention, we can empower individuals to take action and create safer environments for older adults. In this section, we will explore the importance of bystander intervention in detail.

Early Detection and Prevention

Bystanders can often detect signs of elder abuse before it escalates or causes severe harm. By intervening early, they can prevent further abuse and protect the well-being of older adults. Recognizing the signs of elder abuse, such as unexplained injuries, changes in behavior, isolation, or financial exploitation, allows bystanders to take action and seek help promptly. Early intervention can disrupt abusive dynamics, remove victims from harmful situations, and prevent future incidents of abuse.

Creating a Supportive Environment

Bystander intervention contributes to creating a supportive environment where victims of elder abuse feel safe and supported in disclosing their experiences. When bystanders speak up against abuse, it sends a powerful message to victims that they are not alone and that their well-being matters. This supportive environment encourages victims to come forward, seek assistance, and break the silence surrounding their abuse. By creating a culture that prioritizes the safety and dignity of older adults, bystander intervention helps shift societal attitudes towards preventing and addressing elder abuse.

Empowering Victims

Bystander intervention can empower victims of elder abuse by demonstrating that they are not powerless and that help is available. When bystanders intervene, victims may gain the confidence to disclose their experiences, seek assistance, and take steps towards breaking free from abusive situations. Bystanders can provide emotional support, validate the experiences of victims, and connect them with appropriate resources and services. This empowerment helps victims regain control over their lives and contributes to their overall well-being.

Holding Perpetrators Accountable

Bystander intervention plays a crucial role in holding perpetrators of elder abuse accountable for their actions. By speaking out against abuse, bystanders send a clear message that such behavior will not be tolerated. This accountability can deter abusers from continuing their abusive actions and can help break the cycle of abuse within families and communities. Bystander intervention also assists authorities and professionals in gathering evidence and taking appropriate legal actions against the perpetrators.

Education and Awareness

Bystander intervention contributes to the education and awareness about elder abuse within communities. When bystanders take action, they raise awareness among others about the signs, forms, and consequences of elder abuse. This increased awareness helps individuals recognize abusive behaviors, understand the importance of reporting, and take proactive steps to prevent abuse. Bystander intervention also serves as a model for future generations, teaching them the importance of speaking up against injustice and promoting a culture of respect and empathy.

Collaborative Approach

Bystander intervention requires a collaborative approach involving individuals, communities, organizations, and professionals. It fosters a sense of collective responsibility in addressing elder abuse. When bystanders report their concerns or suspicions, it initiates a chain of actions involving law enforcement, healthcare professionals, social services, and legal authorities. This collaborative approach ensures that victims receive the necessary support and intervention, and that abusers are held accountable for their actions.

Prevention of Recurrence

Bystander intervention contributes to preventing the recurrence of elder abuse. When bystanders intervene and report abusive situations, it disrupts the cycle of abuse and sends a message that such behavior will not be tolerated. By addressing the underlying issues that contribute to elder abuse, bystanders can help prevent future incidents and create a safer environment for older adults. Bystander intervention also acts as a deterrent, as potential abusers become aware that their actions may be witnessed and reported by others.

Bystander intervention is a vital component in addressing elder abuse and promoting the safety and well-being of older adults. By recognizing the signs of abuse, intervening early, creating a supportive environment, empowering victims, holding perpetrators accountable, educating communities, and adopting a collaborative approach, bystanders play a crucial role in preventing and addressing elder abuse. Through their actions, bystanders send a powerful message that elder abuse is unacceptable, fostering a culture that values and protects the rights and dignity of older adults.

Confidentiality and legal protections for whistleblowers

Confidentiality and legal protections for whistleblowers are essential safeguards that encourage individuals to come forward with information about wrongdoing, including elder abuse. Whistleblowers play a crucial role in exposing misconduct, advocating for victims, and promoting accountability. By understanding the importance of confidentiality and legal protections, we can create an environment where individuals feel safe and supported when reporting elder abuse. In this section, we will explore the significance of confidentiality and legal protections for whistleblowers in detail.

Confidentiality

Confidentiality is a fundamental principle in whistleblowing that ensures the privacy and protection of individuals who report wrongdoing. It is crucial in cases of elder abuse as it encourages witnesses or victims to come forward without fear of reprisal. The importance of confidentiality in whistleblowing includes

Protection from Retaliation

Confidentiality safeguards whistleblowers from potential retaliation by their employers, colleagues, or the alleged perpetrators. By keeping their identity and information confidential, whistleblowers can report elder abuse without fear of negative consequences to their personal or professional lives.

Encouraging Reporting

Confidentiality creates a safe space for individuals to disclose information about elder abuse. Knowing that their identity will be protected increases the likelihood that witnesses or victims will come forward, enabling a more accurate understanding of the scope and nature of the abuse.

Maintaining Trust

Ensuring confidentiality builds trust between whistleblowers and the entities responsible for receiving and investigating reports. Whistleblowers need assurance that their information will be handled with the utmost care and will not be disclosed without their consent.

Facilitating Investigations

Confidentiality allows investigators to gather information, interview witnesses, and assess the validity of allegations without compromising the identity of the whistleblower. This enables a thorough and unbiased investigation into the reported elder abuse.

Legal Protections for Whistleblowers

Legal protections for whistleblowers are crucial in safeguarding their rights, ensuring their well-being, and encouraging the disclosure of elder abuse. These protections vary across jurisdictions, but common elements include

Anti-Retaliation Measures

Laws often include provisions that prohibit employers from retaliating against whistleblowers who report elder abuse.

Retaliation can take various forms, such as termination, demotion, harassment, or blacklisting. Legal protections ensure that whistleblowers can raise concerns without fear of adverse employment actions.

Confidentiality and Anonymity

Legal frameworks may provide specific provisions to maintain the confidentiality and anonymity of whistleblowers. These protections prevent the disclosure of a whistleblower's identity during investigations or legal proceedings, offering a higher level of security and reducing potential risks.

Whistleblower Hotlines and Reporting Mechanisms

Legislation may require the establishment of whistleblower hotlines or reporting mechanisms to ensure that individuals can report elder abuse safely and confidentially. These channels provide a direct and secure way for whistleblowers to disclose information while protecting their identity.

Legal Remedies and Compensation

Whistleblower protection laws may offer legal remedies and compensation for whistleblowers who experience retaliation or harm as a result of their disclosures. This provides a means for whistleblowers to seek redress if their rights are violated due to their reporting of elder abuse.

Benefits of Confidentiality and Legal Protections

Confidentiality and legal protections for whistleblowers in cases of elder abuse yield several significant benefits, including

Enhanced Reporting

Providing confidentiality and legal protections increases the likelihood of individuals reporting elder abuse. Whistleblowers feel more comfortable coming forward, knowing that their identity and rights will be protected, which enables a more accurate understanding of the extent and nature of elder abuse.

Deterrence of Retaliation

Legal protections deter employers and potential perpetrators from retaliating against whistleblowers. The fear of legal consequences for engaging in retaliation acts encourages a culture of respect, transparency, and accountability.

Encouraging Accountability

Confidentiality and legal protections promote accountability by allowing for thorough investigations into allegations of elder abuse. Whistleblowers' information can be assessed objectively without interference or intimidation, leading to appropriate actions against perpetrators and preventative measures to address systemic issues.

Trust and Confidence

By upholding confidentiality and providing legal protections, organizations demonstrate their commitment to addressing elder abuse and protecting whistleblowers. This fosters trust and confidence in the reporting process, encouraging more individuals to come forward and collaborate in preventing future instances of abuse.

Confidentiality and legal protections are vital elements in whistleblowing related to elder abuse. These safeguards create an environment where witnesses and victims feel safe and supported when reporting abuse. By maintaining confidentiality, whistleblowers are protected from retaliation, enabling them to disclose information without fear of negative consequences. Legal protections further safeguard whistleblowers' rights, ensuring that they are shielded from harm and providing avenues for redress. By upholding confidentiality and implementing robust legal protections, we can encourage whistleblowers to come forward, expose elder abuse, promote accountability, and create safer environments for older adults.

CHAPTER 6
Legal Frameworks: Understanding the Rights and Protections for Seniors

In this chapter, we will explore the legal frameworks that exist to protect the rights of seniors and prevent elder abuse. Understanding these frameworks is essential in promoting the well-being, dignity, and safety of older adults. We will delve into the rights and protections afforded to seniors, the relevant legislation and regulations, and the enforcement mechanisms in place. By comprehending the legal frameworks, we can advocate for the rights of seniors and contribute to the prevention and intervention of elder abuse.

International and Regional Standards

International and regional bodies have established standards and guidelines that outline the rights and protections for seniors. Key instruments include

United Nations Principles for Older Persons

The United Nations Principles for Older Persons highlight the rights of older adults, emphasizing their independence, participation, care, self-fulfillment, and dignity. These principles call for the elimination of discrimination, provision of support services, and access to healthcare, housing, and social security.

Universal Declaration of Human Rights

The Universal Declaration of Human Rights recognizes the inherent dignity and equal rights of all individuals, regardless of age. It establishes the foundation for the protection of seniors' rights, including the right to life, liberty, security, and freedom from abuse or exploitation.

Regional Instruments

Regional bodies, such as the European Union, the Organization of American States, and the African Union, have also developed specific instruments to protect the rights of older adults. These instruments vary by region but generally address issues such as discrimination, social protection, healthcare, and access to justice.

National Legislation and Regulations

Many countries have enacted specific legislation and regulations to protect seniors from abuse and ensure their rights are upheld. Key areas addressed by national legislation include

Elder Abuse Laws

Some countries have enacted laws specifically targeting elder abuse. These laws define elder abuse, establish penalties for offenders, and outline reporting and intervention mechanisms. They may cover various forms of abuse, such as physical, emotional, sexual, financial, and neglect.

Adult Protective Services Laws

Adult protective services laws provide a framework for the prevention and intervention of abuse, neglect, and exploitation of vulnerable adults, including seniors. These laws empower authorities to investigate reports, provide protective services, and coordinate with relevant agencies to ensure the safety and well-being of older adults.

Guardianship and Capacity Laws

Guardianship and capacity laws govern decision-making and the protection of seniors who may lack the capacity to make informed decisions. These laws establish mechanisms to appoint guardians, ensure transparency in decision-making processes, and safeguard the rights and interests of seniors.

Healthcare and Social Welfare Laws

Legislation related to healthcare and social welfare often includes provisions that protect the rights and well-being of seniors. These laws address issues such as access to quality healthcare, long-term care services, social assistance, and the prevention of age discrimination in these sectors.

Enforcement and Reporting Mechanisms

To ensure the effective implementation of legal frameworks, enforcement and reporting mechanisms are crucial. Key elements of enforcement and reporting include

Reporting Mechanisms

Legal frameworks often establish reporting mechanisms for suspected cases of elder abuse. These mechanisms can include hotlines, online reporting portals, or designated agencies responsible for receiving and investigating reports.

Law Enforcement and Legal Remedies

Law enforcement agencies play a crucial role in investigating elder abuse cases, collecting evidence, and pursuing legal action against perpetrators. Legal remedies, such as restraining orders, protective orders, or criminal prosecutions, serve as tools to hold abusers accountable and provide justice to victims.

Regulatory Oversight

Regulatory bodies may oversee the implementation of laws and regulations related to the care and treatment of seniors. These bodies monitor facilities, investigate complaints, and enforce compliance with quality standards to protect the rights and well-being of seniors.

Advocacy and Support Services

Non-governmental organizations, advocacy groups, and support services play a vital role in ensuring seniors' rights are protected. They provide assistance, education, and advocacy on issues related to elder abuse, helping seniors navigate legal processes and access support services.

Understanding the legal frameworks that protect the rights of seniors and prevent elder abuse is crucial in promoting the well-being, dignity, and safety of older adults. International and regional standards, national legislation, and enforcement mechanisms work together to create a framework that upholds the rights of seniors and provides avenues for redress in cases of abuse. By advocating for the implementation and enforcement of these legal frameworks, we can contribute to a society that respects and protects the rights of older adults and works towards preventing and addressing elder abuse.

Legal Frameworks: Understanding the Rights and Protections for Seniors

Laws and regulations governing elder abuse are crucial in protecting older adults from harm, ensuring their rights are upheld, and providing a framework for prevention and intervention. These laws vary across jurisdictions but generally encompass a range of legal measures to address different forms of elder abuse, establish reporting mechanisms, and hold perpetrators accountable. In this section, we will explore the key laws and regulations governing elder abuse, emphasizing the importance of these legal frameworks in safeguarding the well-being and dignity of older adults.

Definition of Elder Abuse

Laws and regulations governing elder abuse typically begin with a clear definition of what constitutes elder abuse. This definition may encompass various forms of abuse, including physical, emotional, sexual, financial, and neglect. Defining elder abuse helps create a common understanding and serves as a basis for legal action and intervention.

Reporting and Intervention Mechanisms

Effective reporting and intervention mechanisms are vital in addressing elder abuse promptly and ensuring the safety of older adults. Laws and regulations provide guidelines for reporting suspected cases of elder abuse, establishing reporting channels such as hotlines, online platforms, or designated agencies responsible for receiving and investigating reports. These mechanisms aim to facilitate timely intervention, protect victims, and gather evidence to hold perpetrators accountable.

Protective Orders and Restraining Orders

Laws and regulations often include provisions for obtaining protective orders or restraining orders in cases of elder abuse. These legal measures serve to safeguard the well-being and safety of older adults by restraining perpetrators from approaching or contacting the victims. Protective orders provide a legal framework to prevent further harm and ensure the physical and emotional security of older adults.

Criminal Penalties

To deter elder abuse and hold perpetrators accountable, laws and regulations impose criminal penalties for those found guilty of committing abuse against older adults. These penalties may vary depending on the severity of the abuse and can include fines, imprisonment, or both. Criminalizing elder abuse sends a strong message that such behavior is unacceptable and may serve as a deterrent for potential abusers.

Financial Protection

Financial abuse is a prevalent form of elder abuse, and laws and regulations often address this issue specifically. They provide safeguards to protect older adults from financial exploitation, scams, undue influence, and mismanagement of their assets. These protections may include measures such as strengthening financial oversight, imposing penalties for financial exploitation, and providing legal remedies for victims.

Long-Term Care Regulations

Laws and regulations governing elder abuse often encompass specific provisions for long-term care facilities, including nursing homes and assisted living facilities. These regulations aim to ensure the quality of care provided, protect the rights of residents, and prevent abuse within these settings. They may include requirements for staff training, resident rights, facility inspections, and complaint investigation processes.

Guardianship and Capacity Laws

Guardianship and capacity laws play a crucial role in protecting older adults who may lack the capacity to make informed decisions or are vulnerable to undue influence. These laws establish mechanisms to appoint guardians when necessary, ensure transparency in decision-making processes, and safeguard the rights and interests of older adults. They provide a legal framework to protect vulnerable seniors from exploitation and abuse.

Mandatory Reporting Obligations

Some jurisdictions have implemented mandatory reporting obligations for professionals who work closely with older adults, such as healthcare providers, social workers, and financial institutions. These laws require professionals to report suspected cases of elder abuse to the appropriate authorities, ensuring that instances of abuse are not overlooked and victims receive the necessary intervention and support.

Training and Education Requirements

Laws and regulations may mandate training and education requirements for professionals who work with older adults to enhance their knowledge and skills in identifying and responding to elder abuse. These requirements ensure that professionals are equipped to recognize the signs of abuse, understand their reporting obligations, and provide appropriate support and intervention to older adults in need.

Non-Discrimination and Ageism

Laws and regulations governing elder abuse often include provisions that prohibit discrimination based on age and promote equality for older adults. These provisions help challenge ageism and ensure that older adults are treated with respect and dignity, regardless of their age or vulnerabilities.

Laws and regulations governing elder abuse are critical in protecting older adults, preventing abuse, and providing avenues for intervention and justice. These legal frameworks define elder abuse, establish reporting and intervention mechanisms, impose criminal penalties, and address specific forms of abuse such as financial exploitation. By advocating for robust legal frameworks, promoting awareness, and ensuring their effective implementation, we can create a society that upholds the rights and well-being of older adults, combats elder abuse, and promotes a culture of respect and dignity for seniors.

Guardianship and conservatorship

Guardianship and conservatorship are legal arrangements that involve the appointment of a guardian or conservator to make decisions on behalf of individuals who are unable to make informed choices due to incapacity or vulnerability. These arrangements aim to protect the rights and interests of individuals who may be at risk of exploitation or neglect. In this section, we will explore the concepts of guardianship and conservatorship, their purposes, and the legal framework surrounding these arrangements.

Guardianship

Guardianship is a legal relationship in which a guardian is appointed by a court to make personal and/or financial decisions for an individual who is deemed incapacitated. The incapacitation may be due to age-related cognitive decline, mental illness, developmental disabilities, or other factors that impair the individual's ability to make decisions in their best interest. The key aspects of guardianship include

Appointment

A guardian is typically appointed through a legal process that involves filing a petition with the court. The court evaluates evidence and determines whether the individual lacks the capacity to make decisions independently. If deemed necessary, the court will appoint a guardian who will assume legal authority to make decisions on behalf of the incapacitated person.

Duties and Powers

The guardian assumes responsibility for making decisions in areas such as healthcare, living arrangements, personal care, and financial matters. The extent of the guardian's powers is determined by the court, and it can range from limited decision-making to full authority over the individual's affairs.

Reporting and Oversight

Guardians are generally required to provide periodic reports to the court detailing the decisions made and the well-being of the individual under their care. The court exercises oversight to ensure that the guardian acts in the best interest of the incapacitated person and does not abuse their authority.

Conservatorship

Conservatorship, also known as guardianship of the estate, focuses specifically on managing the financial affairs and assets of an individual who is unable to manage them independently. The purpose of conservatorship is to protect the individual's financial well-being and prevent financial exploitation. Key aspects of conservatorship include

Appointment

Similar to guardianship, conservatorship requires a court process to appoint a conservator. The court reviews evidence and determines whether the individual is unable to manage their financial affairs due to incapacity or vulnerability. If necessary, a conservator is appointed to oversee and manage the individual's assets.

Financial Management

The conservator assumes responsibility for managing the individual's finances, which may include paying bills, managing investments, filing taxes, and making financial decisions in the best interest of the individual. The conservator is accountable to the court and may be required to seek court approval for significant financial transactions.

Reporting and Oversight

Similar to guardianship, conservators are typically required to provide regular reports to the court, documenting their financial management and the well-being of the individual. The court exercises oversight to ensure the conservator acts in the individual's best interest and does not engage in financial misconduct.

Legal Framework and Safeguards

The legal framework surrounding guardianship and conservatorship varies across jurisdictions, but common elements exist to ensure the protection of individuals' rights and prevent abuse. These safeguards include

Due Process

he legal process for appointing a guardian or conservator includes notice to the individual, an opportunity to be heard, and legal representation. This ensures that the person's rights are respected and that decisions regarding their care and assets are made fairly and transparently.

Least Restrictive Alternatives

Courts typically strive to employ the least restrictive alternatives when considering guardianship or conservatorship. This means exploring other options, such as supported decision-making, power of attorney, or advance directives, before resorting to full guardianship or conservatorship.

Regular Review and Reevaluation

The court periodically reviews guardianship and conservatorship cases to reassess the individual's capacity and the ongoing need for the arrangement. This review process ensures that guardianship and conservatorship remain necessary and that the individual's rights are continually protected.

Conflict of Interest Protections

Guardians and conservators are generally subject to rules and regulations that prevent conflicts of interest and prohibit self-dealing. This prevents abuse of authority and ensures that decisions are made solely in the best interest of the incapacitated person.

Court Oversight and Accountability

Courts exercise oversight to monitor the actions of guardians and conservators, review their reports, and address any concerns or complaints raised by interested parties. This ensures accountability and provides a mechanism for resolving disputes or allegations of misconduct.

Challenges and Criticisms

Guardianship and conservatorship systems have faced criticism and challenges in some jurisdictions. Concerns include potential abuses of power by guardians or conservators, lack of adequate due process, limited alternatives explored before resorting to guardianship, and the potential for individuals' rights to be infringed upon. These challenges have prompted ongoing discussions and efforts to improve the systems, introduce alternatives, and strengthen the safeguards in place.

Guardianship and conservatorship are legal arrangements designed to protect individuals who are unable to make decisions independently due to incapacity or vulnerability. These arrangements provide a framework for decision-making and financial management on behalf of the incapacitated person. While the primary objective is to safeguard the rights and well-being of individuals, it is crucial to ensure that appropriate legal safeguards and oversight mechanisms are in place to prevent abuse and protect individuals' rights. Regular review, transparency, accountability, and exploring least restrictive alternatives are essential to strike a balance between protection and respecting the autonomy and dignity of the individuals under guardianship or conservatorship.

Advance directives and healthcare decision-making

Advance directives and healthcare decision-making are critical components of person-centered care, allowing individuals to express their healthcare preferences and make decisions about their medical treatment in advance. These legal documents and processes ensure that an individual's healthcare wishes are respected, even when they are unable to communicate or make decisions independently. In this section, we will explore advance directives, healthcare decision-making, and their significance in empowering individuals and promoting autonomy in healthcare.

Advance Directives

Advance directives are legal documents that enable individuals to express their healthcare preferences and make decisions about their medical treatment in advance. These directives come into effect when the individual is unable to communicate their wishes due to incapacity or a medical condition. Key types of advance directives include

Living Will

A living will is a written document that outlines an individual's preferences for medical treatment, end-of-life care, and resuscitation efforts. It provides instructions to healthcare providers regarding the use of life-sustaining treatments, such as mechanical ventilation, tube feeding, or cardiopulmonary resuscitation (CPR).

Healthcare Power of Attorney/Proxy

A healthcare power of attorney, also known as a healthcare proxy or surrogate decision-maker, is an individual appointed by the individual to make healthcare decisions on their behalf. The healthcare proxy should be someone trusted by the individual and familiar with their values and wishes.

Do-Not-Resuscitate (DNR) Orders

A Do-Not-Resuscitate (DNR) order is a specific directive that instructs healthcare providers not to perform cardiopulmonary resuscitation (CPR) in the event of cardiac arrest. This order reflects the individual's decision to forgo aggressive resuscitation efforts.

Importance of Advance Directives

Advance directives serve several important purposes and provide numerous benefits, including

Autonomy and Personal Choice

Advance directives empower individuals to maintain control over their healthcare decisions, even when they are unable to communicate. They allow individuals to determine the types of treatment they do or do not want to receive, ensuring their healthcare preferences and values are respected.

Peace of Mind

Having advance directives in place provides individuals and their loved ones with peace of mind, knowing that their wishes regarding medical treatment and end-of-life care are documented and will be honored. This alleviates uncertainty and reduces potential conflicts or disagreements among family members and healthcare providers.

Reducing Burden on Loved Ones

Advance directives relieve the burden on loved ones by clearly articulating the individual's healthcare wishes. This eliminates the need for family members to make difficult decisions in emotionally challenging situations, reducing potential conflicts and ensuring the individual's preferences are upheld.

Consistency in Decision-Making

Advance directives promote consistency in decision-making, ensuring that healthcare providers follow the individual's documented preferences. This is particularly important in cases where family members may have differing opinions or when decisions need to be made quickly in emergency situations.

Respect for Personal Values and Beliefs

Advance directives allow individuals to align their medical treatment decisions with their personal values, cultural beliefs, and religious or spiritual perspectives. This ensures that the healthcare received is in accordance with their deeply held beliefs and maintains their sense of dignity and identity.

Healthcare Decision-Making

Apart from advance directives, healthcare decision-making involves ongoing discussions and processes to ensure that individuals have a voice in their medical treatment. Key elements of healthcare decision-making include

Informed Consent

Informed consent is a fundamental principle in healthcare decision-making. Healthcare providers are required to provide individuals with relevant information about their medical condition, available treatment options, potential risks and benefits, and alternative approaches. Individuals can then make informed decisions about their healthcare based on this information.

Shared Decision-Making

Shared decision-making is a collaborative process between the individual and their healthcare provider. It involves discussing treatment options, considering the individual's values and preferences, and jointly deciding on the most appropriate course of action. Shared decision-making promotes autonomy, patient-centered care, and the integration of medical expertise with individual values and goals.

Surrogate Decision-Making

In cases where individuals are unable to make healthcare decisions or have not appointed a healthcare proxy, surrogate decision-making comes into play. Surrogate decision-makers, usually family members or close friends, make decisions based on their understanding of the individual's preferences and best interests.

Communication and Advance Care Planning

Effective communication between individuals, their families, and healthcare providers is essential in healthcare decision-making. Open and honest discussions about medical conditions, prognosis, treatment options, and individual preferences help ensure that decisions are aligned with the individual's goals and values. Advance care planning involves these conversations and the creation of advance directives to guide future decision-making.

Legal Recognition and Implementation

To ensure the legal recognition and implementation of advance directives and healthcare decision-making, jurisdictions have laws and regulations in place. These laws outline the requirements for creating valid advance directives, clarify the authority of healthcare proxies, and provide guidelines for healthcare providers on honoring advance directives and involving individuals in decision-making.

Advance directives and healthcare decision-making are crucial aspects of person-centered care, empowering individuals to express their healthcare preferences and make decisions about their medical treatment. These legal documents and processes provide autonomy, peace of mind, and consistency in decision-making. By promoting open communication, shared decision-making, and the use of advance directives, we can ensure that individuals' healthcare wishes are respected, even when they are unable to communicate or make decisions independently. It is essential for individuals to engage in advance care planning, discuss their healthcare preferences with loved ones, and create valid advance directives to guide their future medical care.

CHAPTER 7
Preventive Measures Safeguarding Our Loved Ones

In this chapter, we will explore preventive measures that can be implemented to safeguard our loved ones from elder abuse. Prevention is key to ensuring the well-being, dignity, and safety of older adults. By understanding and implementing these preventive measures, we can create environments that promote respect, protect against abuse, and empower individuals. This chapter will delve into various strategies and practices that can be employed to prevent elder abuse effectively.

Education and Awareness

Education and awareness play a vital role in preventing elder abuse. By raising awareness about the signs, types, and consequences of elder abuse, we can equip individuals, families, communities, and professionals with the knowledge needed to recognize and respond to potential abuse. Key aspects of education and awareness include

Public Awareness Campaigns

Initiating public awareness campaigns that highlight the prevalence of elder abuse, its impact on individuals and communities, and the importance of prevention and intervention.

These campaigns can utilize various mediums such as television, radio, social media, and community events to reach a wide audience.

Professional Training

Providing training to healthcare professionals, social workers, caregivers, and other relevant professionals on recognizing and responding to elder abuse. This training should cover topics such as identifying risk factors, effective communication, ethical responsibilities, and reporting procedures.

Community Workshops and Programs

Organizing workshops and programs in community settings to educate older adults, their families, and community members about elder abuse prevention. These initiatives can focus on empowering older adults to protect themselves, understanding their rights, and fostering community support networks.

Empowering Older Adults

Empowering older adults is essential in preventing elder abuse and promoting their well-being. By enhancing their knowledge, self-confidence, and autonomy, we can help older adults protect themselves and make informed decisions. Key elements of empowering older adults include

Rights Awareness

Ensuring that older adults are aware of their rights, including their right to dignity, autonomy, safety, and respect. Educating them about legal protections, available support services, and avenues for reporting abuse empowers them to take action and seek assistance when needed.

Financial Literacy

Providing financial literacy programs to older adults to enhance their understanding of financial management, scams, and fraud prevention. This knowledge equips them with the skills to protect their financial assets and make informed decisions regarding financial matters.

Technology and Digital Literacy

Offering technology and digital literacy programs to older adults, enabling them to navigate online platforms safely, protect their personal information, and detect online scams and exploitation. This empowers them to engage with technology confidently while minimizing risks.

Support Networks and Social Connection

Building strong support networks and fostering social connections for older adults can serve as a preventive measure against elder abuse. These networks provide a sense of belonging, support, and social engagement, reducing social isolation and vulnerability. Key aspects of support networks and social connection include

Community-Based Programs

Establishing community-based programs that facilitate social interaction, such as senior centers, clubs, and interest groups. These programs create opportunities for older adults to connect with peers, engage in activities, and build supportive relationships.

Volunteer and Intergenerational Programs

Encouraging intergenerational programs that foster connections between older adults and younger generations. These programs promote mutual understanding, combat ageism, and reduce isolation for older adults.

Caregiver Support

Providing support services for caregivers, as they play a crucial role in the well-being of older adults. Respite care, counseling, and educational programs can help caregivers manage stress, seek assistance when needed, and ensure quality care for older adults.

Financial Protection

Financial abuse is a significant form of elder abuse, and preventive measures are essential to safeguard older adults' financial well-being. Key elements of financial protection include

Financial Guardianship

Encouraging older adults to designate a trusted individual as a financial power of attorney or establishing a financial guardianship arrangement. This helps protect older adults from financial exploitation and ensures that their financial decisions are made in their best interest.

Scam Awareness

Raising awareness about common scams targeting older adults, such as fraudulent investment schemes, lottery scams, and identity theft. Providing information on scam prevention strategies and promoting skepticism towards unsolicited offers can help older adults protect themselves from financial scams.

Regular Financial Monitoring

Encouraging older adults and their trusted family members or caregivers to regularly monitor financial accounts, statements, and transactions. Timely detection of unusual financial activities can help prevent or minimize the impact of financial abuse.

Collaborative Efforts

Preventing elder abuse requires collaborative efforts among various stakeholders, including government agencies, healthcare professionals, community organizations, and law enforcement. Key aspects of collaborative efforts include

Multi-Disciplinary Teams

Establishing multi-disciplinary teams comprising professionals from different fields, such as social work, healthcare, law enforcement, and legal services. These teams can collaborate to assess complex cases, share information, coordinate interventions, and provide comprehensive support to older adults.

Information Sharing and Communication

Promoting information sharing and communication among professionals and agencies involved in elder abuse prevention and intervention. This facilitates a coordinated response, enables early detection, and ensures efficient service delivery.

Policy and Legislative Initiatives

Advocating for policy and legislative initiatives that prioritize elder abuse prevention, strengthen legal protections, and allocate resources for support services. These initiatives can include funding for education and training programs, improving reporting mechanisms, and enhancing legal frameworks to address emerging forms of elder abuse.

Preventive measures are crucial in safeguarding our loved ones from elder abuse. By implementing education and awareness campaigns, empowering older adults, fostering support networks, promoting financial protection, and fostering collaboration, we can create environments that prevent abuse, promote respect, and empower older adults to live with dignity and safety. It is our collective responsibility to prioritize elder abuse prevention and take proactive measures to ensure the well-being and protection of older adults in our communities.

Education and awareness campaigns

Education and awareness campaigns play a vital role in preventing elder abuse by equipping individuals, families, communities, and professionals with the knowledge and tools to recognize, respond to, and prevent abuse. These campaigns raise awareness about the signs, types, and consequences of elder abuse, promote understanding of the importance of prevention and intervention, and empower individuals to take action. In this section, we will delve into the significance of education and awareness campaigns in preventing elder abuse and explore key elements and strategies for their successful implementation.

Importance of Education and Awareness Campaigns Recognizing Signs of Elder Abuse

Education and awareness campaigns help individuals, including older adults themselves, recognize the signs and symptoms of elder abuse. This includes physical indicators such as unexplained bruises or injuries, behavioral changes, social withdrawal, financial exploitation, or neglect. Increased awareness enables early detection and intervention, potentially preventing further harm.

Promoting Understanding and Knowledge

Education and awareness campaigns provide information about the different types of elder abuse, including physical, emotional, sexual, financial, and neglect. They help individuals understand the dynamics of abuse, its impact on older adults, and the rights and legal protections available. This knowledge empowers individuals to take preventive measures and seek appropriate support.

Empowering Older Adults

Education campaigns specifically targeting older adults empower them to recognize abusive situations, understand their rights, and seek help when needed. By informing them about available support services, reporting mechanisms, and avenues for assistance, older adults are better equipped to protect themselves from abuse and exploitation.

Encouraging Reporting and Intervention

Education and awareness campaigns destigmatize the issue of elder abuse and emphasize the importance of reporting suspected cases. By educating individuals about the appropriate reporting channels and the potential positive outcomes of intervention, campaigns encourage individuals to take action and seek help for themselves or others experiencing abuse.

Challenging Ageism

Education and awareness campaigns challenge ageism by promoting respect, dignity, and equal treatment for older adults. By highlighting the value and contributions of older adults, campaigns strive to change societal attitudes, reduce stereotypes, and create a culture that respects and values the rights of older individuals.

Elements of Effective Education and Awareness Campaigns Clear Messaging

Effective campaigns have clear and concise messaging that is easily understood by various audiences. Campaign materials, including brochures, posters, and videos, should use plain language and visual cues to convey key messages about elder abuse prevention and intervention.

Targeted Approach

Tailoring campaigns to specific audiences is essential for maximum impact. This can include developing materials for older adults, caregivers, healthcare professionals, community members, and law enforcement. Each group may require different information and strategies to address their unique roles in preventing elder abuse.

Multi-Channel Communication

Utilizing multiple communication channels ensures broader reach and increased engagement. This can include traditional methods such as print media, television, and radio, as well as digital platforms like websites, social media, online forums, and email newsletters. Engaging local community organizations, senior centers, and healthcare facilities can also enhance campaign visibility.

Collaboration and Partnerships

Collaborating with key stakeholders, including government agencies, non-profit organizations, healthcare providers, law enforcement, and community groups, strengthens the impact of education and awareness campaigns. Partnering with these entities allows for shared resources, access to expertise, and expanded networks for campaign dissemination.

Culturally and Linguistically Appropriate Materials

Recognizing the diversity within communities, education and awareness campaigns should develop materials that are culturally sensitive and accessible to individuals from diverse backgrounds. This includes using translations, providing materials in multiple languages, and considering cultural nuances in messaging to ensure inclusivity and effective communication.

Evaluation and Feedback

Regular evaluation and feedback are crucial to measure the effectiveness of education and awareness campaigns. Collecting data on campaign reach, audience feedback, and changes in knowledge, attitudes, and behaviors enables campaign organizers to make necessary adjustments, improve future campaigns, and ensure continuous improvement.

Strategies for Effective Education and Awareness Campaigns Community Engagement

Engaging local communities and stakeholders is essential for successful education and awareness campaigns. This can involve organizing community events, workshops, or seminars to raise awareness, share information, and encourage dialogue about elder abuse prevention. Collaborating with community leaders and organizations fosters ownership and support for campaign initiatives.

Professional Training and Continuing Education

Offering professional training programs for healthcare providers, social workers, caregivers, and others who interact with older adults ensures a well-informed network of professionals equipped to recognize and respond to elder abuse. Continuing education opportunities keep professionals updated on best practices and emerging trends in elder abuse prevention.

Storytelling and Personal Testimonials

Sharing real-life stories and personal testimonials of individuals who have experienced elder abuse or successfully intervened in abusive situations can have a powerful impact. These narratives make the issue relatable and provide a human perspective, evoking empathy and encouraging action.

Partnerships with Media

Collaborating with media outlets, including newspapers, television stations, and radio stations, can amplify campaign messages and increase public awareness. Engaging journalists and media professionals to cover stories related to elder abuse prevention, intervention, and support services helps raise public consciousness and visibility.

Integration in Educational Curricula

Incorporating information on elder abuse prevention and intervention into educational curricula at various levels, including schools, colleges, and vocational training programs, ensures that younger generations are exposed to this critical issue. Education in these settings promotes early awareness and establishes a foundation for future advocacy and action.

Education and awareness campaigns are powerful tools in preventing elder abuse. By raising awareness, promoting understanding, and empowering individuals, these campaigns contribute to a society that respects and protects the rights of older adults. Through clear messaging, targeted approaches, collaboration, and community engagement, education and awareness campaigns can effectively reach diverse audiences, challenge ageism, and encourage reporting and intervention. By continuously evaluating and refining these campaigns, we can foster environments that prioritize the prevention of elder abuse, ensuring the well-being, dignity, and safety of our loved ones.

Creating a culture of respect and empathy

Creating a culture of respect and empathy is crucial for promoting the well-being, dignity, and safety of individuals in society. It involves fostering an environment where every person is valued, heard, and treated with compassion. In this section, we will explore the significance of a culture of respect and empathy, its impact on individuals and communities, and strategies for cultivating such a culture.

Understanding a Culture of Respect and Empathy

A culture of respect and empathy goes beyond mere tolerance or politeness. It encompasses an underlying foundation of values and behaviors that prioritize understanding, compassion, and inclusivity. It acknowledges the inherent worth and dignity of every individual, regardless of their age, background, abilities, or differences. Key aspects of a culture of respect and empathy include:

Non-Judgmental Attitudes

A culture of respect and empathy requires individuals to suspend judgment and approach others with an open mind. It involves recognizing that everyone has their own unique experiences, perspectives, and challenges, and that these differences should be acknowledged and respected.

Active Listening

Actively listening to others is an essential component of empathy and respect. It involves giving one's full attention, showing genuine interest, and seeking to understand the thoughts, feelings, and experiences of others without interruption or preconceived notions. Active listening fosters connection and validates the experiences of individuals.

Empathy and Compassion

Cultivating empathy and compassion involves the ability to understand and share the emotions and experiences of others. It requires putting oneself in another person's shoes, recognizing their feelings, and responding with kindness and support. Empathy helps create a sense of belonging and fosters mutual respect.

Inclusivity and Valuing Diversity

A culture of respect and empathy celebrates diversity and recognizes the richness that different perspectives, backgrounds, and experiences bring to society. It actively includes and values individuals from all walks of life, promoting equality, fairness, and justice.

Impact of a Culture of Respect and Empathy Personal Well-being

A culture of respect and empathy has a positive impact on individuals' well-being. When individuals are treated with respect and empathy, they feel valued, heard, and understood. This fosters self-esteem, emotional well-being, and mental health, promoting a sense of belonging and acceptance.

Enhanced Relationships

Respect and empathy form the foundation of healthy and positive relationships. When individuals feel respected and understood, it nurtures trust, strengthens communication, and fosters deeper connections with others. This applies to relationships within families, communities, workplaces, and broader society.

Reduced Conflict and Violence

A culture of respect and empathy helps mitigate conflicts and reduce instances of violence. When individuals engage in respectful communication, seek to understand one another, and practice empathy, it promotes dialogue, cooperation, and peaceful resolution of differences. This contributes to a safer and more harmonious community.

Social Cohesion and Solidarity

A culture of respect and empathy promotes social cohesion and solidarity within communities. When individuals respect and empathize with one another, it fosters a sense of collective responsibility, encourages collaboration, and strengthens social bonds. This leads to stronger communities that work together for the well-being of all members.

Prevention of Abuse and Discrimination

A culture of respect and empathy acts as a preventive measure against abuse and discrimination. When individuals are respectful and empathetic, they are less likely to engage in abusive behavior or perpetuate discriminatory attitudes. This creates a safer environment for vulnerable individuals, including older adults, by fostering a sense of safety, trust, and protection.

Strategies for Cultivating a Culture of Respect and Empathy Education and Awareness

Education plays a vital role in cultivating a culture of respect and empathy. Promoting education programs that emphasize values such as respect, empathy, and inclusivity in schools, workplaces, and community settings helps instill these principles from an early age. It fosters an understanding of the importance of these values and equips individuals with the necessary skills to practice them.

Role Modeling

Leaders, parents, educators, and influential figures in society have a significant role to play in shaping a culture of respect and empathy. By modeling respectful and empathetic behavior in their interactions, they set an example for others to follow. Positive role models can inspire individuals to cultivate these qualities in their own lives and relationships.

Promoting Active Listening

Encouraging active listening skills helps individuals develop empathy and respect for others. Providing training, workshops, or resources that focus on active listening techniques helps individuals become better listeners, fostering understanding, connection, and mutual respect.

Encouraging Dialogue and Collaboration

Creating spaces for open dialogue and collaboration enables individuals to engage in meaningful conversations, exchange ideas, and challenge biases and stereotypes. These opportunities for dialogue promote empathy, broaden perspectives, and foster a culture of respect and understanding.

Creating Supportive Policies and Practices

Establishing policies and practices that prioritize respect, empathy, and inclusivity creates a supportive environment in various settings, including workplaces, schools, healthcare facilities, and community organizations. These policies can include diversity and inclusion initiatives, anti-discrimination measures, and conflict resolution processes that promote respectful communication and equitable treatment.

Community Engagement and Partnerships

Engaging the community and forming partnerships with local organizations, non-profits, and community leaders strengthens the collective effort to cultivate a culture of respect and empathy. Collaborative initiatives, events, and awareness campaigns can be organized to promote understanding, empathy, and respect for all community members.

Creating a culture of respect and empathy is essential for the well-being and harmony of individuals and communities. It requires a commitment to practicing empathy, fostering inclusive attitudes, and valuing the inherent worth of every individual. By promoting education, active listening, dialogue, and supportive policies, we can foster a culture that respects and values diversity, promotes understanding, and cultivates empathy. Through these efforts, we can create a society where every individual feels heard, understood, and treated with dignity and compassion.

Building strong support networks for seniors

Building strong support networks for seniors is essential for promoting their overall well-being, reducing social isolation, and enhancing their quality of life. These networks provide emotional support, social connections, and practical assistance, ensuring that seniors feel valued, connected, and supported in their communities. In this section, we will explore the significance of strong support networks for seniors, the benefits they offer, and strategies for building and maintaining these networks.

Importance of Support Networks for Seniors Emotional Support

Support networks offer emotional support to seniors, providing a sense of belonging, companionship, and understanding. This support helps combat feelings of loneliness, depression, and anxiety that often accompany social isolation in older adults. Having individuals who listen, empathize, and offer encouragement can significantly enhance seniors' mental and emotional well-being.

Social Engagement

Strong support networks facilitate social engagement, enabling seniors to participate in social activities, maintain friendships, and connect with others who share their interests and experiences. Social interaction is crucial for combating social isolation and maintaining cognitive function, as it stimulates conversation, intellectual engagement, and a sense of purpose.

Physical Assistance

Support networks can also offer practical assistance to seniors in carrying out daily activities, such as grocery shopping, transportation, or household chores. This assistance promotes independence, reduces the risk of falls or accidents, and ensures that seniors can age in place with the necessary support.

Information and Resources

Support networks provide access to valuable information and resources that can help seniors navigate healthcare services, financial matters, legal concerns, and other aspects of their lives. These networks can connect seniors to organizations, agencies, and professionals who specialize in addressing the unique needs of older adults.

Advocacy and Empowerment

Strong support networks empower seniors by advocating for their rights, needs, and interests. These networks can raise awareness about issues affecting seniors, challenge ageism, and actively engage in efforts to improve policies and services that impact the aging population. Seniors who are part of supportive networks often feel empowered, valued, and influential in shaping their own lives and communities.

Strategies for Building Strong Support Networks for Seniors Community Engagement

Encouraging seniors to engage with their local communities is vital for building support networks. Community centers, senior centers, and organizations dedicated to older adult services offer various programs, activities, and social gatherings that foster connections among seniors. These platforms provide opportunities for seniors to meet and interact with others who share their interests.

Intergenerational Programs

Intergenerational programs bring together individuals of different ages, allowing seniors to build relationships with younger generations. These programs can involve mentoring, volunteering, or joint activities that promote mutual learning, understanding, and companionship. Intergenerational connections help combat ageism, reduce isolation, and provide meaningful social interactions for seniors.

Peer Support Groups

Facilitating peer support groups specifically designed for seniors allows individuals to connect with others who share similar experiences or challenges. These groups can focus on specific topics, such as health conditions, caregiving, grief, or hobbies. Peer support groups provide a safe space for seniors to share, learn from one another, and provide mutual support.

Volunteer Opportunities

Encouraging seniors to engage in volunteer activities not only benefits the community but also helps them build social connections and a sense of purpose. Volunteer organizations often offer a range of opportunities tailored to seniors' abilities and interests, allowing them to contribute their skills, knowledge, and time to meaningful causes.

Technology and Digital Connectivity

Embracing technology and digital connectivity can enhance seniors' access to support networks. Training programs and workshops can help older adults develop digital literacy skills, enabling them to connect with others through social media, online forums, and video calls. Virtual support groups and online communities can provide valuable connections, especially for seniors with limited mobility or geographical constraints.

Family and Friends

Building and maintaining strong relationships with family members and friends is crucial for seniors' support networks. Encouraging regular communication, organizing family gatherings, and fostering intergenerational connections strengthen bonds and provide a reliable support system for seniors.

Maintaining Strong Support Networks for Seniors Regular Communication

Consistent communication within support networks is essential for maintaining strong connections. Encouraging phone calls, visits, or video chats with network members helps seniors stay engaged, informed, and emotionally connected.

Continuing Education

Promoting opportunities for seniors to engage in lifelong learning, such as classes, workshops, or discussion groups, ensures that they continue to grow intellectually and remain connected to their communities. Lifelong learning fosters engagement and helps seniors maintain an active role within their support networks.

Regular Social Activities

Organizing regular social activities, outings, or events within support networks keeps seniors connected and engaged. These activities can include game nights, book clubs, exercise classes, or outings to cultural or recreational venues. Regular gatherings provide opportunities for social interaction and foster a sense of camaraderie.

Accessibility and Inclusivity

Ensuring that support networks are accessible and inclusive to all seniors, regardless of their abilities, mobility, or cultural backgrounds, is essential. Consideration should be given to physical accessibility of venues, providing transportation options, offering multilingual resources, and embracing cultural diversity within support networks.

Training and Education

Providing training and education opportunities to network members, including family members, friends, and professionals, ensures that they have the necessary knowledge and skills to support seniors effectively. Training can focus on topics such as communication techniques, understanding aging-related issues, and addressing the specific needs of seniors.

Building strong support networks for seniors is vital for their overall well-being, social engagement, and quality of life. These networks offer emotional support, social connections, practical assistance, and advocacy, promoting seniors' sense of belonging and empowering them to age with dignity and independence. By implementing strategies such as community engagement, intergenerational programs, peer support groups, and embracing technology, we can create robust support networks that help combat social isolation, enhance seniors' quality of life, and ensure that they remain connected, valued, and supported in their communities.

Chapter 8
Empowering Caregivers: Training and Support for Quality Care

In this chapter, we will explore the importance of empowering caregivers through training and support to ensure the delivery of quality care. Caregivers play a critical role in supporting the well-being and daily needs of individuals who require assistance due to age, illness, or disability. By providing caregivers with the necessary knowledge, skills, and resources, we can enhance their ability to provide compassionate and effective care. This chapter will delve into the significance of caregiver empowerment, the benefits it brings to both caregivers and care recipients, and strategies for training and supporting caregivers.

The Significance of Caregiver Empowerment Enhanced Care Quality

Empowering caregivers through training and support leads to improved care quality for individuals receiving assistance. Caregivers who are equipped with the necessary skills and knowledge can provide personalized, safe, and effective care. This includes understanding and addressing the physical, emotional, and social needs of care recipients, implementing proper care techniques, and promoting overall well-being.

Increased Confidence and Job Satisfaction

Caregivers who receive comprehensive training and ongoing support experience increased confidence in their abilities. This confidence translates into job satisfaction, as caregivers feel more competent, valued, and fulfilled in their roles. Empowered caregivers are more likely to provide compassionate care, which positively impacts the emotional well-being of both caregivers and care recipients.

Reduced Caregiver Burnout

Caregiving can be physically and emotionally demanding, leading to caregiver burnout and increased stress levels. Empowering caregivers through training and support equips them with coping mechanisms, self-care strategies, and resources to manage their own well-being. This, in turn, reduces burnout, enhances resilience, and ensures the sustainability of caregiving relationships.

Improved Communication and Collaboration

Empowered caregivers are better equipped to communicate effectively with care recipients, their families, and healthcare professionals. This includes listening attentively, advocating for the needs of care recipients, and actively participating in care planning and decision-making processes. Improved communication and collaboration result in more coordinated and person-centered care.

Strategies for Caregiver Training and Support Comprehensive Initial Training

Providing caregivers with comprehensive initial training is essential for equipping them with fundamental knowledge and skills. Training programs can cover various aspects of caregiving, including proper techniques for personal care, medication management, safety protocols, and understanding specific conditions or disabilities. These programs should also address the psychological and emotional aspects of caregiving, such as empathy, active listening, and managing caregiver stress.

Ongoing Education and Skill Development

Caregivers should have access to ongoing education and skill development opportunities to enhance their knowledge and expertise. This can involve workshops, webinars, online courses, or in-service training sessions that focus on emerging best practices, new research, and advancements in care techniques. Continuous learning ensures that caregivers stay updated and can provide the best possible care.

Emotional and Psychological Support

Caregivers often face emotional challenges, stress, and grief associated with their roles. Providing access to counseling services, support groups, or mental health resources can help caregivers navigate these challenges and cope with the emotional demands of caregiving. Emotional support promotes caregiver well-being and resilience, enabling them to provide better care.

Peer Support Networks

Establishing peer support networks allows caregivers to connect with others who share similar experiences. Peer support networks provide a platform for caregivers to share insights, seek advice, and find emotional support. These networks can be facilitated through support groups, online forums, or community-based caregiver organizations.

Respite Care

Respite care offers caregivers temporary relief by providing them with time off from their caregiving responsibilities. This can be in the form of in-home respite care, adult day programs, or short-term residential respite care. Respite care allows caregivers to rest, recharge, and attend to their own needs, reducing the risk of burnout and ensuring the sustainability of caregiving relationships.

Access to Resources and Information

Caregivers should have access to resources, information, and referral services that can assist them in their caregiving journey. This may include access to relevant websites, helplines, educational materials, and community resources that provide guidance on navigating the caregiving process, accessing support services, and understanding available benefits and entitlements.

Recognition and Appreciation

Recognizing and appreciating the contributions of caregivers is crucial for their empowerment and morale. This can involve acknowledging their efforts through formal appreciation events, certificates, or public recognition. Creating a culture within organizations and communities that values and appreciates caregivers helps to promote their well-being and encourages them to continue providing quality care.

Empowering caregivers through training and support is essential for ensuring the delivery of quality care to individuals in need. By equipping caregivers with the necessary knowledge, skills, and resources, we can enhance their ability to provide compassionate and effective care. Comprehensive training, ongoing education, emotional support, and access to resources are all critical elements of caregiver empowerment. By investing in caregiver training and support, we not only improve the well-being and job satisfaction of caregivers but also enhance the overall quality of care provided to care recipients. Caregivers are vital partners in the healthcare system, and it is our collective responsibility to empower them to provide the best possible care to those who depend on their support.

Caregiver burnout and stress management

Caregiver burnout and stress management are essential aspects of supporting the well-being of caregivers who provide care for individuals in need. Caregiving can be physically and emotionally demanding, often leading to chronic stress, exhaustion, and feelings of overwhelm. It is crucial to address caregiver burnout and provide effective stress management strategies to ensure the sustainability of caregiving relationships and maintain the overall well-being of caregivers. In this section, we will explore caregiver burnout, its causes and consequences, and strategies for managing stress and preventing burnout.

Understanding Caregiver Burnout Causes of Caregiver Burnout

Caregiver burnout can arise from various factors, including the physical demands of caregiving, emotional strain, lack of support, financial challenges, and the overall impact of assuming responsibility for someone's well-being. Caregivers may experience burnout when they consistently prioritize the needs of others while neglecting their own well-being.

Signs and Symptoms of Caregiver Burnout

Caregiver burnout manifests in various ways, and recognizing its signs and symptoms is crucial for early intervention. Common signs include chronic fatigue, sleep disturbances, feelings of overwhelm or helplessness, increased irritability or mood swings, withdrawal from social activities, neglecting personal self-care, and physical health problems. These symptoms can significantly impact the caregiver's overall well-being and quality of life.

Consequences of Caregiver Burnout

Caregiver burnout can have detrimental effects on both the caregiver and the care recipient. It can lead to increased risk of depression, anxiety, and other mental health issues for caregivers. Additionally, burnout can compromise the quality of care provided, as exhausted and overwhelmed caregivers may struggle to meet the needs of the care recipient effectively.

Strategies for Managing Caregiver Stress and Preventing Burnout Self-Care Practices

Encouraging caregivers to prioritize self-care is essential for managing stress and preventing burnout. This includes engaging in activities that promote relaxation, such as exercise, meditation, hobbies, or spending time in nature. Adequate sleep, proper nutrition, and maintaining a healthy lifestyle are also crucial components of self-care.

Seeking Emotional Support

Caregivers should be encouraged to seek emotional support to cope with the challenges they face. This can involve connecting with friends and family members, joining caregiver support groups, or seeking professional counseling. Sharing experiences, concerns, and emotions with others who understand can provide validation, empathy, and a sense of community.

Respite Care

Respite care provides caregivers with a temporary break from their caregiving responsibilities. It can involve arranging for a qualified caregiver to step in or utilizing respite care services, such as adult day programs or short-term residential care. Respite care allows caregivers to recharge, attend to their own needs, and prevent burnout.

Time Management and Prioritization

Effective time management and prioritization can help caregivers maintain balance and prevent overwhelm. Caregivers should be encouraged to set realistic expectations, delegate tasks when possible, and establish boundaries to ensure they have time for their own needs and interests.

Accessing Support Services

Caregivers should be aware of and connected to support services available in their communities. These may include home healthcare services, meal delivery programs, transportation assistance, and support from local caregiver organizations. Utilizing these services can alleviate some of the caregiving responsibilities and provide valuable assistance.

Developing Coping Strategies

Caregivers can benefit from developing coping strategies to manage stress and maintain their well-being. This can involve deep breathing exercises, journaling, practicing mindfulness, engaging in creative outlets, or participating in stress reduction programs.

Coping strategies empower caregivers to navigate challenges effectively and build resilience.

Effective Communication and Setting Boundaries

Clear and open communication is crucial in caregiving relationships. Caregivers should feel comfortable expressing their needs, concerns, and limitations to the care recipient and other family members involved in the care. Setting boundaries, both with the care recipient and with other responsibilities, helps maintain a healthy balance and prevent caregiver burnout.

Seeking Professional Assistance

Caregivers should not hesitate to seek professional assistance when needed. This may involve consulting healthcare professionals, social workers, or geriatric care managers who can provide guidance, resources, and specialized support for caregivers and care recipients.

Addressing caregiver burnout and providing effective stress management strategies are crucial for supporting the well-being of caregivers. Caregiving can be physically and emotionally challenging, and caregivers often neglect their own needs while prioritizing the care of others. By implementing self-care practices, seeking emotional support, utilizing respite care, managing time effectively, accessing support services, developing coping strategies, and setting boundaries, caregivers can better manage stress and prevent burnout. Caregivers play a vital role in supporting the well-being of individuals in need, and it is crucial to ensure their own well-being and sustainability in their caregiving roles. By providing caregivers with the necessary support and resources, we can empower them to continue providing compassionate and effective care while maintaining their own health and well-being.

Training programs for professional and family caregivers

Training programs for professional and family caregivers are instrumental in equipping individuals with the necessary knowledge, skills, and resources to provide effective and compassionate care. These programs are designed to address the unique challenges and demands of caregiving, enhancing the quality of care provided and promoting the well-being of both caregivers and care recipients. In this section, we will explore the importance of training programs for professional and family caregivers, the benefits they offer, and key components to consider in their development and implementation.

Importance of Training Programs for Professional and Family Caregivers Enhanced Care Quality

Training programs equip caregivers with the knowledge and skills needed to provide high-quality care. They ensure that caregivers have a solid understanding of best practices in areas such as personal care, medication management, safety protocols, and disease-specific care. By enhancing care quality, training programs contribute to better health outcomes and overall well-being for care recipients.

Increased Confidence and Competence

Training programs boost caregivers' confidence and competence in their roles. By providing them with a strong foundation of knowledge and skills, caregivers feel more capable and empowered to handle the challenges that caregiving presents.

This increased confidence positively impacts their ability to provide compassionate and effective care.

Effective Communication and Empathy

Training programs emphasize the importance of effective communication and empathy in caregiving. Caregivers learn to listen actively, express empathy, and communicate clearly with care recipients, family members, and healthcare professionals. These skills foster trust, understanding, and positive relationships, enhancing the overall caregiving experience.

Safety and Risk Management

Training programs emphasize safety protocols and risk management strategies. Caregivers learn how to identify potential hazards, prevent accidents, and respond effectively to emergencies. This knowledge ensures the safety and well-being of care recipients and minimizes the risk of injury or harm.

Emotional and Psychological Support

Training programs address the emotional and psychological aspects of caregiving. Caregivers learn how to manage stress, cope with caregiver burnout, and prioritize self-care. This support is crucial for caregivers to maintain their own well-being and provide compassionate care while navigating the emotional challenges associated with caregiving.

Key Components of Training Programs for Professional and Family Caregivers Fundamental Skills and Knowledge

Training programs should cover fundamental caregiving skills and knowledge, such as personal hygiene, mobility assistance, medication management, infection control, and recognizing signs of distress or illness. These foundational elements ensure caregivers have a solid understanding of the essentials of caregiving.

Disease-Specific Care

Caregivers may require specialized training when caring for individuals with specific conditions or diseases. Disease-specific training programs provide in-depth knowledge about the particular needs, symptoms, and challenges associated with those conditions. Examples include dementia care, diabetes management, or palliative care.

Communication and Empathy

Effective communication and empathy are critical components of caregiving. Training programs should focus on developing active listening skills, effective communication techniques, and strategies for expressing empathy and understanding. These skills enable caregivers to establish positive relationships with care recipients and their families.

Safety and Risk Management

Training programs should address safety protocols and risk management strategies to ensure the well-being of both caregivers and care recipients. This includes training on fall prevention, safe transfer techniques, infection control, medication safety, and emergency preparedness.

Caregiver Self-Care and Stress Management

Caregivers need to prioritize self-care and manage their own well-being. Training programs should emphasize the importance of self-care and provide strategies for stress management, resilience-building, and seeking support. This ensures that caregivers can maintain their own health and well-being while providing care to others.

Cultural Competence

Caregivers interact with individuals from diverse cultural backgrounds. Training programs should promote cultural competence by raising awareness of cultural differences, addressing biases, and providing strategies for delivering culturally sensitive care. This fosters respectful and inclusive care practices.

Legal and Ethical Considerations

Caregivers need to be aware of legal and ethical considerations in caregiving. Training programs should provide guidance on privacy and confidentiality, informed consent, advance care planning, and ethical decision-making. This ensures that caregivers navigate their roles in a legally and ethically responsible manner.

Implementation of Training Programs Tailored Content

Training programs should be tailored to the specific needs of professional and family caregivers. This includes considering the target audience, their level of experience, and the unique challenges they may face in their caregiving roles.

Interactive and Practical Approach

Training programs should employ interactive and practical teaching methods to engage learners. This can include role-playing, case studies, hands-on demonstrations, and opportunities for skill practice. Interactive approaches enhance learning and facilitate the application of knowledge in real-world caregiving situations.

Continuous Education

Caregiving is an evolving field, and training programs should promote continuous education and professional development. This can include refresher courses, ongoing workshops, or access to online resources and support networks. Continuous education ensures that caregivers stay updated on best practices and emerging trends in caregiving.

Collaboration and Partnerships

Training programs should collaborate with healthcare institutions, community organizations, and caregiving support networks. These collaborations facilitate access to resources, foster shared learning, and create a network of support for caregivers. Partnerships also enable a multidisciplinary approach to caregiving training, incorporating perspectives from various healthcare professionals.

Training programs for professional and family caregivers are essential for enhancing care quality, promoting caregiver confidence and competence, and ensuring the well-being of both caregivers and care recipients. By addressing fundamental caregiving skills, disease-specific care, effective communication, safety protocols, caregiver self-care, and legal and ethical considerations, these programs equip caregivers with the knowledge and skills needed to provide compassionate and effective care. Implementation of tailored, interactive, and continuous training programs, along with collaboration and partnerships, helps create a strong support system for caregivers. By investing in caregiver training and support, we can empower caregivers to deliver quality care while prioritizing their own well-being, ultimately enhancing the overall caregiving experience and improving the lives of those in their care.

Resources and assistance for caregivers

Resources and assistance for caregivers are vital in providing support, guidance, and practical help to individuals who assume caregiving responsibilities for their loved ones. Caregiving can be challenging, both physically and emotionally, and caregivers often require resources and assistance to navigate their roles effectively while maintaining their own well-being. In this section, we will explore the importance of resources and assistance for caregivers, the benefits they offer, and various types of support available.

Importance of Resources and Assistance for Caregivers Information and Guidance

Caregivers need access to reliable information and guidance to understand the specific needs and challenges of the individuals they care for. Resources provide essential information on caregiving techniques, disease-specific care, medication management, legal and financial matters, and available support services. Access to accurate information empowers caregivers to make informed decisions and provide the best possible care.

Emotional Support

Caregiving can be emotionally demanding, and caregivers often require emotional support to cope with stress, frustration, and feelings of isolation. Emotional support resources provide a space for caregivers to share their experiences, connect with others facing similar challenges, and seek empathy, validation, and encouragement. Such support helps caregivers navigate the emotional aspects of caregiving, reducing feelings of burden and promoting well-being.

Practical Assistance

Caregivers often face practical challenges, such as managing daily tasks, coordinating appointments, and finding respite care options. Resources that offer practical assistance provide guidance on organizing caregiving schedules, accessing transportation services, finding home healthcare providers, and exploring respite care programs. These resources help alleviate the logistical burdens of caregiving, ensuring that caregivers can focus on providing quality care.

Education and Training

Caregivers benefit from resources that offer education and training opportunities to enhance their knowledge and skills. Educational resources provide access to webinars, workshops, online courses, and printed materials that cover various caregiving topics, including communication strategies, disease-specific care, safety precautions, and self-care practices. Education and training empower caregivers to deliver competent and effective care.

Financial and Legal Guidance

Caregivers may face financial and legal challenges related to caregiving. Resources that offer financial and legal guidance provide information on available benefits and entitlements, long-term care insurance, estate planning, and legal considerations related to caregiving, such as power of attorney and advance directives. This support helps caregivers navigate the complex financial and legal aspects of caregiving, reducing stress and ensuring financial stability.

Types of Resources and Assistance for Caregivers
Caregiver Support Groups

Support groups bring together caregivers facing similar challenges, providing a safe space for sharing experiences, discussing concerns, and offering mutual support. These groups can be in-person or online, facilitated by professionals or peer-led, and may focus on specific conditions or caregiving topics.

Helplines and Hotlines

Helplines and hotlines offer caregivers access to immediate support, guidance, and information. Trained professionals are available to answer questions, provide emotional support, offer crisis intervention, and refer caregivers to appropriate resources or services.

Respite Care Programs

Respite care programs provide temporary relief to caregivers by offering professional care for their loved ones. This allows caregivers to take a break, attend to personal needs, and recharge. Respite care can be provided in-home, at adult day centers, or through short-term residential care.

Caregiver Websites and Online Communities

Caregiver-specific websites and online communities provide a wealth of information, educational resources, and forums for caregivers to connect with others. These platforms offer access to articles, webinars, discussion boards, and expert advice, allowing caregivers to access support and information from the comfort of their homes.

Caregiver Training Programs

Caregiver training programs provide education and skills development opportunities to enhance caregivers' knowledge and competence. These programs may be offered by healthcare institutions, community organizations, or online platforms. Training programs cover various caregiving topics, including disease-specific care, communication skills, safety protocols, and self-care practices.

Caregiver Resource Centers

Caregiver resource centers serve as central hubs for information, referrals, and support services. These centers provide caregivers with access to resource libraries, support groups, educational programs, and connections to community resources, including respite care services and financial assistance programs.

Government and Nonprofit Organizations

Government and nonprofit organizations offer a range of resources and assistance for caregivers. These organizations may provide information on available support services, financial aid programs, caregiver training, and respite care options. They can also advocate for caregiver rights, policy changes, and increased funding for caregiver support initiatives.

Professional Caregiver Services

Professional caregiver services can provide trained and qualified individuals to assist with caregiving tasks, such as personal care, medication management, and household chores. These services offer peace of mind to caregivers, ensuring that their loved ones receive quality care when additional support is needed.

Resources and assistance for caregivers are essential for providing support, guidance, and practical help to individuals in their caregiving roles. Access to information, emotional support, practical assistance, education and training, and financial and legal guidance empowers caregivers to navigate the challenges of caregiving effectively while maintaining their own well-being. By utilizing available resources and seeking assistance from various support networks, caregivers can provide quality care, reduce feelings of isolation, and enhance their own resilience and satisfaction in their caregiving journey. It is crucial for governments, organizations, and communities to continue developing and expanding resources and assistance programs to meet the evolving needs of caregivers and recognize their invaluable contributions.

CHAPTER 9
Healing and Recovery: Rehabilitation for Abuse Survivors

In this chapter, we will explore the importance of healing and recovery through rehabilitation for abuse survivors. Survivors of abuse, whether it is physical, emotional, sexual, or financial, often face profound physical and psychological trauma. Rehabilitation programs aim to support survivors in their journey towards healing, recovery, and reclaiming their lives. This chapter will delve into the significance of rehabilitation for abuse survivors, the principles underlying effective rehabilitation, and the various components of a comprehensive rehabilitation program.

Importance of Rehabilitation for Abuse Survivors Physical Healing

Many abuse survivors suffer from physical injuries and health complications as a result of the abuse they have endured. Rehabilitation programs provide access to medical care, physical therapy, and other specialized interventions to address physical injuries, promote healing, and restore functional abilities. Physical healing is crucial for survivors to regain their physical well-being and restore their sense of agency.

Emotional and Psychological Recovery

Abuse survivors often experience significant emotional and psychological trauma, including anxiety, depression, post-traumatic stress disorder (PTSD), and complex trauma. Rehabilitation programs offer specialized counseling, therapy, and mental health support to address these psychological wounds. By providing a safe and supportive environment, survivors can process their emotions, develop coping strategies, and rebuild their self-esteem and resilience.

Empowerment and Reclaiming Autonomy

Abuse can strip survivors of their sense of control and autonomy. Rehabilitation programs focus on empowering survivors by helping them regain a sense of agency over their lives. This involves providing education, skills training, and support to develop their self-confidence, assertiveness, and decision-making abilities. Empowerment helps survivors rebuild their lives on their terms and move forward with a renewed sense of purpose and independence.

Rebuilding Relationships and Trust

Abuse often damages survivors' ability to trust others and form healthy relationships. Rehabilitation programs offer support in rebuilding social connections, fostering healthy relationships, and addressing any relationship difficulties resulting from the abuse. Through group therapy, family counseling, and support networks, survivors can learn to develop trusting relationships and establish a support system that contributes to their healing process.

Principles of Effective Rehabilitation for Abuse Survivors
Trauma-Informed Approach

Effective rehabilitation programs adopt a trauma-informed approach, recognizing the impact of trauma on survivors and providing services that are sensitive to their unique needs. This approach involves creating a safe and respectful environment, promoting trust, and empowering survivors in their recovery journey.

Holistic Care

Rehabilitation programs should address the multidimensional needs of abuse survivors. This includes addressing physical, emotional, psychological, and social aspects of healing. A holistic approach ensures that survivors receive comprehensive support that recognizes and addresses the interconnected nature of their experiences.

Individualized Treatment Plans

Each survivor's journey of healing is unique, and effective rehabilitation programs develop individualized treatment plans based on the survivor's specific needs and goals. These plans consider factors such as the type and severity of abuse, cultural background, personal preferences, and existing strengths. Individualized treatment plans ensure that survivors receive tailored support and interventions that best meet their needs.

Collaboration and Interdisciplinary Care

Rehabilitation programs should involve a multidisciplinary team of professionals, including psychologists, counselors, medical providers, social workers, and other specialists. Collaborative care allows for comprehensive assessment, treatment planning, and coordination of services. This interdisciplinary approach ensures that survivors receive holistic care and support from a range of experts.

Components of a Comprehensive Rehabilitation Program for Abuse Survivors Individual and Group Therapy

Individual therapy offers survivors a safe space to explore their experiences, emotions, and beliefs. Group therapy provides a supportive environment where survivors can connect with others who have had similar experiences, share their stories, and gain validation and support from peers.

Trauma-Focused Counseling

Trauma-focused counseling approaches, such as Cognitive-Behavioral Therapy (CBT) and Eye Movement Desensitization and Reprocessing (EMDR), help survivors process traumatic experiences, develop coping strategies, and reduce the impact of trauma-related symptoms.

Medical and Physical Care

Rehabilitation programs should provide access to medical and physical care, including medical examinations, treatment of physical injuries, pain management, and rehabilitation services such as physiotherapy or occupational therapy. This ensures survivors' physical well-being and promotes their overall recovery.

Psychoeducation and Skills Training

Psychoeducation equips survivors with knowledge about the impact of abuse, common trauma responses, and coping strategies. Skills training focuses on developing skills such as assertiveness, communication, emotional regulation, self-care, and boundary-setting. These skills empower survivors to navigate their daily lives and build resilience.

Social Support and Community Engagement

Rehabilitation programs facilitate social support through support groups, peer mentoring, and community-based activities. Engaging with supportive communities and participating in meaningful activities help survivors rebuild social connections, develop a sense of belonging, and reduce feelings of isolation.

Legal Advocacy and Support

Many abuse survivors navigate legal processes, such as filing reports or seeking protection orders. Rehabilitation programs may provide access to legal advocacy services, offering survivors guidance, support, and referrals to legal professionals experienced in handling abuse cases.

Aftercare and Follow-up Support

Rehabilitation programs should include aftercare services and follow-up support to ensure that survivors continue to receive the necessary assistance even after the program concludes. This may involve providing access to ongoing therapy, support groups, and referrals to community resources.

Rehabilitation plays a crucial role in supporting the healing and recovery of abuse survivors. By addressing physical healing, emotional and psychological recovery, empowerment, and rebuilding relationships, rehabilitation programs provide survivors with the necessary tools, support, and resources to reclaim their lives. A comprehensive rehabilitation program, guided by trauma-informed principles, incorporates individualized treatment plans, collaboration among professionals, and a range of interventions to meet survivors' unique needs. Through rehabilitation, abuse survivors can embark on a path towards healing, rediscover their resilience and self-worth, and regain control over their lives.

Healing and Recovery Rehabilitation for Abuse Survivors

Physical and emotional recovery for abused elders is a critical aspect of their healing journey. Elder abuse, whether it is physical, emotional, sexual, or financial, can have devastating effects on the well-being and dignity of older individuals. Rehabilitation programs and interventions specifically tailored to address the physical and emotional needs of abused elders play a vital role in their recovery. In this section, we will explore the importance of physical and emotional recovery for abused elders, the challenges they may face, and the strategies and interventions that can support their healing process.

Physical Recovery for Abused Elders Medical Assessment and Treatment

Physical recovery begins with a comprehensive medical assessment to identify and address any immediate injuries or health concerns resulting from the abuse. Medical professionals, including geriatric specialists and forensic nurses, can conduct thorough examinations, provide necessary treatments, and address medical conditions exacerbated by the abuse.

Rehabilitation Services

Abused elders may require rehabilitation services to regain or improve their physical functioning and mobility. These services can include physical therapy, occupational therapy, and speech therapy, depending on the specific needs and goals of the individual. Rehabilitation helps elders rebuild their strength, regain independence in daily activities, and improve their overall quality of life.

Pain Management

Many abused elders experience physical pain as a result of the abuse they have endured. Pain management strategies, including medication, physical therapies, and alternative approaches like acupuncture or massage, can help alleviate their pain and improve their comfort and well-being.

Assistive Devices and Home Modifications

Abused elders may benefit from the use of assistive devices such as canes, walkers, or wheelchairs to enhance their mobility and safety. Additionally, home modifications, such as installing handrails or ramps, can create a more accessible and supportive environment for their physical recovery.

Nutritional Support

Ensuring proper nutrition is crucial for the physical recovery of abused elders. Nutritionists or dietitians can assess the individual's dietary needs and develop personalized meal plans to promote healing, maintain a healthy weight, and address any nutritional deficiencies resulting from the abuse.

Emotional Recovery for Abused Elders Trauma-Informed Counseling

Abused elders often experience significant emotional trauma, including anxiety, depression, post-traumatic stress disorder (PTSD), and feelings of shame or guilt. Trauma-informed counseling, provided by trained professionals experienced in working with older adults, focuses on creating a safe and supportive environment. It helps abused elders process their emotions, heal from the trauma, and develop coping strategies to manage distressing symptoms.

Support Groups

Joining support groups specifically tailored for abused elders can be beneficial in their emotional recovery process. These groups provide a space for elders to connect with others who have had similar experiences, share their stories, offer mutual support, and learn from each other's coping mechanisms and resilience. Support groups foster a sense of belonging, validation, and empowerment.

Expressive Therapies

Expressive therapies, such as art therapy, music therapy, or dance therapy, can be effective in supporting the emotional recovery of abused elders. These creative approaches provide non-verbal avenues for self-expression, emotional release, and exploring difficult emotions in a safe and supportive environment.

Cognitive-Behavioral Therapy (CBT)

CBT is a therapeutic approach widely used in treating emotional trauma and related conditions. It helps abused elders challenge negative thought patterns, develop healthier coping strategies, and reframe their experiences. CBT promotes emotional resilience, positive self-esteem, and improved overall mental well-being.

Mindfulness and Relaxation Techniques

Mindfulness and relaxation techniques, such as meditation, deep breathing exercises, or guided imagery, can assist abused elders in managing stress, reducing anxiety, and promoting emotional well-being. These practices help elders cultivate a sense of calm, increase self-awareness, and develop resilience in the face of emotional challenges.

Social Support and Meaningful Connections

Maintaining and nurturing social connections is crucial for the emotional recovery of abused elders. Engaging in social activities, participating in community programs, and spending time with loved ones or supportive friends can help combat isolation, improve self-esteem, and provide a sense of belonging and purpose.

Physical and emotional recovery for abused elders is a complex and multifaceted process that requires tailored interventions and support. By addressing the physical needs through medical assessment, rehabilitation services, pain management, assistive devices, and nutritional support, abused elders can regain their physical functioning and well-being. Emotional recovery, facilitated through trauma-informed counseling, support groups, expressive therapies, CBT, mindfulness practices, and social connections, helps abused elders heal from the emotional trauma they have experienced and rebuild their emotional well-being and resilience. Recognizing the unique challenges faced by abused elders and providing comprehensive and compassionate care are essential in supporting their journey towards physical and emotional recovery, promoting their dignity, and enhancing their overall quality of life.

Counseling and therapy options

Counseling and therapy options play a crucial role in supporting individuals facing various challenges, including those who have experienced abuse. Counseling and therapy provide a safe and supportive environment for individuals to explore their thoughts, emotions, and experiences, facilitating healing, personal growth, and overall well-being. In this section, we will delve into different counseling and therapy options, explaining their approaches, benefits, and suitability for individuals who have experienced abuse.

Individual Counseling

Individual counseling involves one-on-one sessions between a trained therapist and the individual seeking support. It offers a confidential space for individuals to share their experiences, express their emotions, and work through their challenges in a personalized and tailored manner. Individual counseling can be particularly beneficial for individuals who have experienced abuse, as it provides a safe and non-judgmental environment to process trauma, explore underlying issues, and develop coping strategies.

Cognitive-Behavioral Therapy (CBT)

CBT focuses on identifying and challenging negative thought patterns and beliefs that contribute to distressing emotions and behaviors. It helps individuals develop healthier cognitive patterns and learn practical skills to manage their emotions and cope with difficult situations. CBT is often effective in addressing the impact of trauma, managing anxiety and depression, and enhancing overall well-being.

Trauma-Focused Therapy

Trauma-focused therapy, such as Eye Movement Desensitization and Reprocessing (EMDR) or Trauma-Focused Cognitive-Behavioral Therapy (TF-CBT), is specifically designed to address the impact of trauma on individuals. These therapies help individuals process traumatic memories, reduce distressing symptoms, and develop effective coping strategies. Trauma-focused therapy can be highly beneficial for individuals who have experienced abuse, as it focuses on their unique trauma-related needs.

Psychodynamic Therapy

Psychodynamic therapy explores unconscious patterns and unresolved conflicts that may contribute to emotional distress. Through exploring past experiences and their impact on current emotions and behaviors, psychodynamic therapy aims to increase self-awareness and facilitate personal growth. It can be helpful for individuals who have experienced abuse, as it provides a deeper understanding of the underlying dynamics and their impact on the individual's well-being.

Person-Centered Therapy

Person-centered therapy emphasizes the therapeutic relationship and focuses on the individual's inherent capacity for growth and self-actualization. The therapist provides a supportive and non-directive environment, encouraging individuals to explore their own feelings and experiences. Person-centered therapy can be beneficial for individuals who have experienced abuse, as it promotes self-empowerment and self-acceptance.

Group Therapy

Group therapy involves individuals with similar experiences or challenges coming together in a facilitated group setting to share their experiences, provide support, and learn from one another. Group therapy can be a valuable option for individuals who have experienced abuse, as it provides a sense of belonging, validation, and connection with others who have had similar experiences.

Support Groups

Support groups for abuse survivors offer a safe and supportive space for individuals to share their stories, express their emotions, and receive validation and support from others who have had similar experiences. Support groups foster a sense of community, reduce feelings of isolation, and provide an opportunity for learning coping strategies and resilience-building.

Psychoeducational Groups

Psychoeducational groups focus on providing information, education, and skill-building related to specific issues or challenges. In the context of abuse, psychoeducational groups may provide information about the effects of abuse, healthy coping mechanisms, self-care strategies, and empowerment. These groups help individuals develop knowledge and skills to navigate the healing process and enhance their overall well-being.

Family Therapy

Family therapy involves the participation of family members in therapy sessions to address relational dynamics, improve communication, and promote understanding and healing within the family unit. Family therapy can be beneficial for individuals who have experienced abuse, as it provides a platform to address the impact of the abuse on family relationships, facilitate open dialogue, and foster a supportive and healthy family environment.

Trauma-Informed Family Therapy

Trauma-informed family therapy focuses on understanding the impact of trauma on family dynamics and relationships. It aims to improve communication, rebuild trust, and strengthen the overall family system. Trauma-informed family therapy recognizes the unique needs of abuse survivors and provides a safe space for family members to process the impact of the abuse and work together towards healing and recovery.

Online Counseling and Teletherapy

Online counseling, also known as teletherapy or e-counseling, provides counseling and therapy services through digital platforms, such as video conferencing or secure messaging. Online counseling can be a convenient and accessible option for individuals who may have difficulty accessing in-person sessions due to various reasons, such as geographical distance or physical limitations. It allows individuals to receive professional support and therapy from the comfort of their own homes, while still maintaining confidentiality and privacy.

Counseling and therapy options offer valuable support to individuals who have experienced abuse. Through individual counseling, group therapy, family therapy, and online counseling, individuals can access safe and supportive environments to process their experiences, heal from trauma, develop coping strategies, and enhance their overall well-being. The various therapeutic approaches, such as CBT, trauma-focused therapy, and person-centered therapy, cater to different needs and preferences. It is important for individuals who have experienced abuse to work with qualified and experienced therapists who specialize in trauma and abuse-related issues. By seeking professional help and engaging in counseling and therapy, individuals who have experienced abuse can embark on a healing journey towards personal growth, resilience, and reclaiming their lives.

Rebuilding trust and restoring dignity

Rebuilding trust and restoring dignity are essential aspects of the healing process for individuals who have experienced abuse. Abuse, whether it is physical, emotional, sexual, or financial, can shatter a person's sense of trust in others and deeply impact their self-worth and dignity. In this section, we will explore the importance of rebuilding trust and restoring dignity, the challenges that may arise, and strategies and interventions to support individuals in their journey towards regaining trust and reclaiming their inherent worth.

Rebuilding Trust Establishing Safety

Rebuilding trust begins with creating a safe and secure environment for individuals who have experienced abuse. It is crucial to ensure their physical and emotional safety and provide assurances that they will not be subjected to further harm. Establishing safety allows individuals to gradually develop a sense of trust in their surroundings and the people around them.

Consistency and Reliability

Consistency and reliability in words and actions are key elements in rebuilding trust. It is essential to follow through on commitments, demonstrate dependability, and act consistently over time. This helps individuals develop confidence in others' integrity and sincerity.

Transparency and Open Communication

Transparent and open communication fosters trust by promoting honesty, clarity, and mutual understanding. Encouraging individuals to express their concerns, feelings, and needs in a safe and supportive environment helps build trust. Active listening, validation, and empathy play crucial roles in promoting effective communication and rebuilding trust.

Setting Boundaries

Respecting personal boundaries is vital in rebuilding trust. Individuals who have experienced abuse may have had their boundaries violated. It is important to create an environment that recognizes and respects their autonomy, consent, and personal space. By establishing and respecting boundaries, trust can gradually be rebuilt.

Trust-Building Activities

Engaging in trust-building activities can help individuals gradually develop trust in themselves and others. These activities may involve teamwork, problem-solving exercises, or shared experiences that foster cooperation, reliability, and mutual support. Participating in such activities allows individuals to witness and experience trustworthy behaviors, promoting the gradual rebuilding of trust.

Restoring Dignity

Validation and Empowerment: Restoring dignity involves recognizing and validating the experiences, feelings, and worth of individuals who have experienced abuse. It is important to affirm their inherent value, strengths, and resilience. Providing opportunities for empowerment, such as decision-making, autonomy, and participation in their own healing journey, helps restore a sense of dignity and agency.

Trauma-Informed Care

Adopting a trauma-informed approach is crucial in restoring dignity for individuals who have experienced abuse. This approach recognizes the impact of trauma on an individual's well-being and emphasizes safety, trustworthiness, choice, collaboration, and empowerment. Trauma-informed care ensures that the dignity and unique needs of each individual are respected throughout the healing process.

Self-Care and Self-Compassion

Encouraging self-care and self-compassion is essential in restoring dignity. Individuals who have experienced abuse may struggle with feelings of shame, guilt, or self-blame. Promoting self-care practices, such as engaging in activities that bring joy, setting boundaries, and prioritizing physical and emotional well-being, supports the restoration of dignity and self-worth.

Building Positive Relationships

Building positive, supportive relationships is instrumental in restoring dignity. Surrounding individuals with caring, empathetic, and respectful individuals helps counteract the negative impact of past abusive relationships. Positive relationships provide opportunities for healthy connections, validation, and the experience of being treated with dignity and respect.

Engaging in Meaningful Activities

Engaging in meaningful activities that align with personal values, interests, and goals contributes to the restoration of dignity. Participation in activities that promote personal growth, creativity, community engagement, or contribution to others helps individuals regain a sense of purpose, self-esteem, and a positive identity beyond their experiences of abuse.

Professional Support: Counseling and Therapy

Counseling and therapy, tailored to address the specific needs of individuals who have experienced abuse, can be instrumental in supporting the journey towards rebuilding trust and restoring dignity. Therapists experienced in trauma and abuse-related issues provide a safe and supportive space to explore the impact of abuse, process emotions, develop coping strategies, and cultivate resilience.

Support Groups

Joining support groups specifically designed for abuse survivors can provide individuals with a sense of community, validation, and shared experiences. Support groups offer opportunities for connecting with others who have gone through similar challenges, receiving support, and learning from one another's journeys towards regaining trust and restoring dignity.

Rebuilding trust and restoring dignity are essential components of the healing process for individuals who have experienced abuse. Creating a safe and supportive environment, promoting consistent and trustworthy behaviors, encouraging open communication, and engaging in trust-building activities facilitate the gradual restoration of trust. Similarly, validating experiences, empowering individuals, adopting a trauma-informed approach, promoting self-care and self-compassion, building positive relationships, and accessing professional support contribute to restoring dignity. By recognizing the inherent worth and resilience of individuals who have experienced abuse and providing the necessary support and interventions, we can assist them in regaining trust in others and themselves, reclaiming their dignity, and moving towards a future of healing and personal growth.

CHAPTER 10
Creating a Brighter Future: Advocacy and Policy Changes

In this chapter, we will explore the importance of advocacy and policy changes in creating a brighter future for individuals who have experienced abuse. Advocacy involves raising awareness, promoting change, and influencing policies and practices to prevent abuse, protect survivors, and ensure their access to justice and support. Policy changes are crucial in establishing legal frameworks, guidelines, and resources that prioritize the rights, safety, and well-being of abuse survivors. This chapter will delve into the significance of advocacy and policy changes, the key areas that require attention, and the strategies for creating a brighter future for survivors.

Raising Awareness

Advocacy efforts must begin with raising awareness about the prevalence and impact of abuse. By disseminating information through campaigns, community events, educational programs, and media platforms, awareness can be increased among the general public, professionals, and policymakers. Raising awareness helps combat the stigma surrounding abuse, encourages open dialogue, and promotes a culture of support and accountability.

Prevention Strategies

Advocacy should focus on implementing prevention strategies to address the root causes of abuse. Prevention efforts may include

Education and Training

Promoting education and training programs that equip individuals, professionals, and communities with knowledge about abuse, its warning signs, and prevention strategies. This includes training for healthcare providers, educators, law enforcement personnel, and community leaders.

Promoting Healthy Relationships

Encouraging healthy relationship dynamics, consent, empathy, and respect through awareness campaigns, educational curricula, and community initiatives. Promoting healthy relationships reduces the likelihood of abuse and fosters a culture of respect and equality.

Early Intervention Programs

Implementing early intervention programs that identify and address risk factors, provide support services, and empower individuals to intervene and report abuse. These programs can be implemented in schools, workplaces, healthcare settings, and community organizations.

Survivor Support and Access to Justice

Advocacy efforts must prioritize survivor support and access to justice, ensuring that survivors have the necessary resources, services, and legal protections to seek justice and rebuild their lives. Key areas of focus include

Support Services

Advocating for accessible and comprehensive support services, such as counseling, medical care, crisis hotlines, and shelter options. These services should be tailored to the unique needs of abuse survivors, including culturally sensitive and trauma-informed approaches.

Legal Reforms

Advocating for legal reforms that enhance the legal protections for abuse survivors, including stronger legislation, simplified reporting processes, and specialized courts or legal services dedicated to handling abuse cases. Legal reforms should prioritize survivor safety, confidentiality, and their rights throughout legal proceedings.

Empowering Survivor Voices

Advocating for survivor voices to be heard and respected in all stages of the justice system. This includes providing opportunities for survivors to share their experiences, participate in policy discussions, and contribute to the development of guidelines and practices.

Collaborative Efforts

Collaborating with legal professionals, victim advocates, healthcare providers, social service agencies, and community organizations to ensure a coordinated and multidisciplinary approach to survivor support and access to justice. Collaboration promotes comprehensive care, information sharing, and efficient service delivery.

Funding and Resources

Advocacy involves advocating for increased funding and resources to support abuse prevention, survivor support services, research, and training initiatives. Adequate funding ensures the availability of quality services, enhances prevention efforts, and supports innovative approaches to addressing abuse.

Policy Changes

Advocacy efforts should aim to influence policy changes at various levels, including local, national, and international. Key policy changes may include:

Strengthening Laws and Regulations

Advocating for the development and strengthening of laws and regulations that criminalize abuse, establish clear guidelines for reporting and investigation, and provide comprehensive protections for survivors.

Mandatory Reporting

Advocating for the implementation of mandatory reporting laws across sectors, such as healthcare, education, and social services, to ensure that abuse is promptly reported and appropriate interventions are implemented.

Improved Training and Standards

Advocating for improved training programs and standards for professionals who work with abuse survivors, such as healthcare providers, law enforcement personnel, and social workers. Training should focus on recognizing and responding to abuse, trauma-informed approaches, and cultural competence.

Collaborative Policies

Advocating for policies that promote collaboration among different sectors, such as healthcare, legal, and social services, to ensure a coordinated response to abuse cases. This includes establishing multidisciplinary teams, information-sharing protocols, and interagency cooperation.

Data Collection and Research

Advocating for the collection of comprehensive data on elder abuse, including prevalence rates, risk factors, and impact. This data can inform policy decisions, resource allocation, and the development of evidence-based interventions.

Advocacy and policy changes play a vital role in creating a brighter future for individuals who have experienced abuse. By raising awareness, implementing prevention strategies, prioritizing survivor support and access to justice, advocating for funding and resources, and influencing policy changes, advocates can promote a culture of accountability, prevention, and support. Through collaborative efforts and a focus on survivor empowerment, advocacy can contribute to a society where abuse is prevented, survivors are supported, and the rights and dignity of all individuals are upheld. Creating a brighter future requires ongoing commitment, collaboration, and a collective effort to effect meaningful change and ensure a safer and more just society for all.

Legislative efforts to combat elder abuse

Legislative efforts to combat elder abuse are crucial in establishing legal frameworks and protections to prevent, detect, and respond to abuse against older individuals. Legislation plays a vital role in holding perpetrators accountable, ensuring access to justice for survivors, and providing resources and support for prevention and intervention initiatives. In this section, we will explore the importance of legislative efforts, key areas of focus, and specific legislative measures to combat elder abuse.

Importance of Legislative Efforts

Legislative efforts are vital in addressing elder abuse for several reasons

Establishing Legal Protections

Legislation defines and establishes legal protections for older adults, ensuring that their rights are safeguarded and that perpetrators can be held accountable for their actions. By clearly defining different forms of elder abuse, legislators can create a foundation for effective prevention and response strategies.

Promoting Prevention and Education

Legislation can facilitate the development and implementation of prevention programs and educational initiatives. Through legislation, governments can allocate resources, establish guidelines, and mandate educational campaigns aimed at raising awareness about elder abuse, promoting healthy aging, and equipping individuals with knowledge and skills to prevent abuse.

Enhancing Reporting and Investigation

Legislative efforts can simplify and streamline the reporting and investigation processes, making it easier for individuals to report abuse and for authorities to investigate cases. By implementing mandatory reporting laws and establishing protocols for interagency cooperation, legislation ensures that abuse is promptly reported and addressed.

Improving Support Services

Legislation can provide the framework for the establishment and funding of support services for elder abuse survivors. This includes funding for counseling, emergency shelters, legal assistance, and victim advocacy services. Legislative measures can also address barriers to accessing services, such as transportation, language, or cultural barriers, to ensure that support is accessible to all survivors.

Enhancing Legal Remedies

Legislative efforts can expand legal remedies available to elder abuse survivors, such as restraining orders, protective orders, and emergency guardianship. These measures aim to provide immediate protection for survivors and empower them to seek legal recourse against their abusers.

Key Areas of Focus for Legislative Efforts

Legislative efforts to combat elder abuse should focus on the following key areas

Definitions and Classifications

Legislation should provide clear definitions and classifications of different forms of elder abuse, including physical, emotional, sexual, and financial abuse, as well as neglect and self-neglect. Clear definitions help professionals and the public understand the scope of abuse and facilitate appropriate responses.

Reporting and Mandatory Reporting Laws

Legislation should establish reporting requirements for professionals who work closely with older adults, such as healthcare providers, social workers, and financial institutions. Mandatory reporting laws ensure that abuse is promptly reported and that professionals fulfill their legal obligations to protect older individuals.

Legal Protections and Penalties

Legislation should establish legal protections for older adults, including enhanced penalties for perpetrators of elder abuse. These protections may include criminalizing specific acts of abuse, establishing civil remedies for survivors, and imposing sanctions on institutions that fail to protect older individuals from abuse.

Support Services and Resources

Legislation should allocate funding and resources to support services specifically designed for elder abuse survivors. This includes funding for counseling, emergency shelters, legal aid, and financial assistance programs. Legislative efforts should also prioritize culturally sensitive and trauma-informed services that address the unique needs of older survivors.

Specific Legislative Measures to Combat Elder Abuse

Legislative efforts to combat elder abuse can encompass a range of specific measures, such as

Elder Abuse Prevention and Awareness Programs

Legislation can mandate the development and implementation of elder abuse prevention and awareness programs, including educational campaigns, community outreach initiatives, and training for professionals who work with older adults.

Guardianship and Conservatorship Reforms

Legislation can establish guidelines and oversight mechanisms for guardianships and conservatorships to prevent abuse and exploitation. Reforms may include background checks for potential guardians, regular monitoring of guardian activities, and mechanisms for removing abusive or negligent guardians.

Mandatory Background Checks

Legislation can require mandatory background checks for individuals working in positions of trust and responsibility, such as caregivers, nursing home staff, and employees of home care agencies. Background checks help identify individuals with a history of abuse or neglect and prevent their employment in positions that involve caregiving responsibilities.

Financial Protections

Legislation can enhance financial protections for older adults by criminalizing financial exploitation, regulating power of attorney arrangements, and establishing mechanisms for reporting and investigating financial abuse cases. These measures aim to prevent financial abuse and provide avenues for legal recourse for survivors.

Collaboration and Coordination

Legislation can promote collaboration and coordination among different agencies and sectors involved in preventing and addressing elder abuse. This includes establishing multidisciplinary teams, information-sharing protocols, and interagency cooperation to ensure a coordinated response to abuse cases.

Legislative efforts are crucial in combatting elder abuse and protecting the rights and well-being of older adults. By establishing legal protections, promoting prevention and education, enhancing reporting and investigation processes, improving support services, and expanding legal remedies, legislation creates a framework for effective prevention, intervention, and justice for elder abuse survivors. Legislative measures should prioritize the unique needs of older individuals, cultural sensitivity, and trauma-informed approaches. Through robust legislative efforts and ongoing commitment to combating elder abuse, societies can work towards creating safer environments and a brighter future for older adults.

Strengthening elder protection agencies and law enforcement

Strengthening elder protection agencies and law enforcement is critical in effectively combating elder abuse and ensuring the safety and well-being of older adults. Elder protection agencies and law enforcement play pivotal roles in preventing abuse, investigating reported cases, and providing support and justice for elder abuse survivors. In this section, we will delve into the importance of strengthening these entities, key areas of focus, and strategies to enhance their effectiveness in addressing elder abuse.

Importance of Strengthening Elder Protection Agencies and Law Enforcement: Prevention and Education

Strong elder protection agencies and law enforcement can actively engage in prevention and education initiatives. They can raise awareness about elder abuse, disseminate information about available resources and support services, and educate the public, professionals, and older adults themselves on recognizing and reporting abuse. Prevention efforts can help address risk factors, promote early intervention, and foster a culture of accountability and respect for older adults.

Reporting and Investigation

Strengthened elder protection agencies and law enforcement can establish efficient systems for reporting and investigating elder abuse cases. Streamlining reporting processes, ensuring prompt response to reports, and conducting thorough investigations are crucial in holding perpetrators accountable and providing justice for survivors. Robust investigative techniques, including specialized training on elder abuse, forensic protocols, and collaboration with other professionals, can enhance the effectiveness of investigations.

Support and Services

Strong elder protection agencies can provide comprehensive support services for elder abuse survivors. This includes offering crisis intervention, counseling, legal assistance, case management, and referrals to appropriate resources. Collaborating with community organizations, healthcare providers, and social service agencies can facilitate a coordinated response, ensuring that survivors have access to the necessary support and services to aid their recovery.

Data Collection and Research

Strengthening elder protection agencies and law enforcement includes enhancing data collection and research efforts. Collecting accurate and comprehensive data on the prevalence, types, and consequences of elder abuse can inform policy decisions, resource allocation, and the development of targeted interventions. Research can help identify risk factors, evaluate the effectiveness of prevention programs, and contribute to the overall understanding of elder abuse dynamics.

Key Areas of Focus for Strengthening Elder Protection Agencies and Law Enforcement

Specialized Training

Providing specialized training to law enforcement officers, investigators, and elder protection agency staff is essential. Training should cover topics such as recognizing signs of abuse, conducting sensitive interviews, trauma-informed approaches, and legal aspects specific to elder abuse cases. Ongoing professional development ensures that personnel are equipped with the necessary knowledge and skills to effectively respond to elder abuse cases.

Collaboration and Multidisciplinary Approach

Strengthening collaboration among elder protection agencies, law enforcement, healthcare providers, social service agencies, and legal professionals is crucial. Establishing multidisciplinary teams or task forces can facilitate information-sharing, joint investigations, and coordinated responses to cases. This collaborative approach ensures that the unique needs of elder abuse survivors are met through a comprehensive and integrated system of care.

Resource Allocation

Adequate resource allocation is essential to strengthen elder protection agencies and law enforcement. This includes funding for personnel training, specialized units or divisions focused on elder abuse, technological resources for data management and analysis, and support services for survivors. Sufficient resources allow agencies and law enforcement to carry out their responsibilities effectively and efficiently.

Public-Private Partnerships

Engaging in partnerships with private entities, such as financial institutions, businesses, and community organizations, can strengthen elder protection efforts. Partnerships can involve training programs, awareness campaigns, financial education initiatives, and collaboration in reporting and investigating financial abuse cases. By working together, public and private sectors can maximize their impact in safeguarding older adults.

Strategies to Enhance Effectiveness

Public Awareness Campaigns: Elder protection agencies and law enforcement can conduct public awareness campaigns to educate the community about elder abuse, its signs, and the importance of reporting. These campaigns can also promote collaboration between agencies and community members in preventing and addressing elder abuse.

Community Engagement

Strengthening relationships with community organizations, advocacy groups, and local stakeholders is crucial. Regular engagement with these entities fosters community support, promotes information sharing, and enhances collaboration in addressing elder abuse.

Technological Advancements

Embracing technological advancements can improve the efficiency and effectiveness of elder protection agencies and law enforcement. This can include implementing digital reporting systems, utilizing data analytics for identifying trends and patterns, and leveraging online platforms for educational resources and awareness campaigns.

Legislative Support

Advocating for legislative support is essential in strengthening elder protection efforts. This includes advocating for dedicated funding, enhanced legal protections, and the development of specific legislation to address emerging challenges in elder abuse.

Strengthening elder protection agencies and law enforcement is crucial in effectively combating elder abuse and ensuring the safety and well-being of older adults. By focusing on prevention, efficient reporting and investigation, comprehensive support services, and robust data collection, these entities can contribute to a society where older adults are protected and abuse is prevented. Collaboration, specialized training, resource allocation, public-private partnerships, and legislative support are key strategies to enhance the effectiveness of elder protection agencies and law enforcement. Together, these efforts create a stronger and more responsive system that empowers older adults, holds abusers accountable, and promotes a culture of respect and dignity for older individuals.

Promoting systemic changes in elder care

Promoting systemic changes in elder care is crucial for ensuring the well-being, safety, and dignity of older adults. Systemic changes involve addressing the underlying structures, policies, and practices within the elder care system to create a more person-centered, inclusive, and comprehensive approach to care. In this section, we will explore the importance of systemic changes in elder care, key areas that require attention, and strategies for promoting these changes.

Importance of Systemic Changes in Elder Care

Person-Centered Care: Systemic changes aim to shift the focus of elder care from a one-size-fits-all approach to person-centered care. This approach recognizes the individuality, preferences, and needs of older adults, promoting their active participation in decision-making, care planning, and goal-setting. Person-centered care enhances quality of life, autonomy, and dignity for older adults.

Prevention of Abuse and Neglect

Systemic changes can strengthen measures to prevent abuse, neglect, and exploitation within the elder care system. This includes implementing stringent background checks for caregivers, ensuring adequate staffing levels, establishing comprehensive training programs, and enhancing oversight and monitoring mechanisms. By prioritizing prevention, systemic changes promote a safe and secure environment for older adults.

Integration of Health and Social Care

Systemic changes aim to integrate health and social care services to provide holistic and coordinated support for older adults. This involves breaking down silos between different service providers, such as healthcare professionals, social workers, and community organizations, to ensure seamless delivery of care. Integrated care improves outcomes, reduces fragmentation, and enhances the overall well-being of older adults.

Caregiver Support and Training

Systemic changes recognize the importance of caregiver support and training. This includes providing caregivers with the necessary resources, education, and training to enhance their skills, knowledge, and well-being. Supportive measures for caregivers, such as respite care, counseling services, and financial assistance, can help alleviate caregiver burden and promote high-quality care for older adults.

Key Areas Requiring Systemic Changes: Workforce Development

Systemic changes should focus on workforce development within the elder care sector. This includes attracting and retaining skilled professionals, ensuring adequate staffing levels, offering competitive wages and benefits, and providing ongoing training and professional development opportunities. A well-trained and supported workforce is essential for delivering high-quality care to older adults.

Aging in Place

Systemic changes should support the concept of aging in place, allowing older adults to live independently in their own homes or communities for as long as possible. This involves investing in home and community-based services, improving accessibility and safety modifications, and promoting social connections and support networks. Aging in place enhances older adults' autonomy, social engagement, and overall well-being.

Technology and Innovation

Systemic changes should embrace the use of technology and innovation to improve elder care. This includes implementing electronic health records, telehealth services, assistive technologies, and remote monitoring systems. Technology can enhance communication, coordination of care, access to services, and health outcomes for older adults.

Advocacy and Policy Reform

Systemic changes require advocacy and policy reform at local, national, and international levels. Advocacy efforts should focus on highlighting the needs and rights of older adults, promoting person-centered care, and influencing policy decisions to allocate resources and prioritize elder care. Policy reforms should address gaps and inconsistencies in regulations, promote best practices, and ensure the protection of older adults' rights and well-being.

Strategies for Promoting Systemic Changes Collaboration and Partnerships

Promoting systemic changes requires collaboration among stakeholders, including government agencies, healthcare providers, social service organizations, advocacy groups, and older adults themselves. Collaboration fosters knowledge sharing, leverages resources, and amplifies the collective voice to drive systemic changes.

Research and Evidence-Based Practice

Systemic changes should be informed by research and evidence-based practices. Conducting research on best practices, evaluating outcomes of interventions, and disseminating knowledge are crucial for driving systemic changes and implementing effective policies and practices in elder care.

Public Awareness and Education

Promoting systemic changes necessitates raising public awareness about the needs, challenges, and rights of older adults. This includes educating the public about ageism, elder abuse, and the importance of person-centered care. Public awareness campaigns can help mobilize support, advocate for policy changes, and promote a societal shift towards valuing and respecting older adults.

Policy Advocacy

Advocacy efforts should focus on influencing policy decisions at various levels. This involves engaging with policymakers, participating in public consultations, and advocating for legislative reforms that prioritize the well-being, safety, and dignity of older adults. Policy advocacy amplifies the voices of older adults and ensures that their concerns are reflected in policy and legislative changes.

Promoting systemic changes in elder care is essential for creating a more person-centered, inclusive, and comprehensive approach to caring for older adults. By focusing on person-centered care, prevention of abuse and neglect, integration of health and social care, and support for caregivers, systemic changes can enhance the quality of care and well-being of older adults. Workforce development, aging in place, technology and innovation, advocacy and policy reform, collaboration, research, public awareness, and policy advocacy are key strategies for driving these changes. By implementing systemic changes, we can create an elder care system that respects the rights and dignity of older adults, promotes their well-being, and ensures a better future for aging populations.

Taking a Stand Together a Call to Action

Throughout this book, we have delved into the hidden horrors of elder abuse, exposing its various forms and shedding light on the vulnerable state of our loved ones. We have explored the importance of recognizing the signs, understanding the profiles of abusers, and uncovering the settings prone to abuse. We have emphasized the significance of reporting, intervention, and the legal frameworks that protect seniors. We have discussed preventive measures, the empowerment of caregivers, the rehabilitation of abuse survivors, and the need for systemic changes in elder care. Now, as we conclude this journey, we are presented with a call to action—a call to take a stand together against elder abuse.

Elder abuse is not an isolated issue

it is a societal problem that requires a collective response. Each and every one of us has a role to play in creating a safer and more respectful environment for our loved ones as they age. It is not enough to be aware of the issue; we must actively engage in prevention, intervention, and advocacy efforts. It is time to step up, raise our voices, and make a difference.

Taking a stand against elder abuse starts with education and awareness. We must educate ourselves and others about the signs of abuse, the rights of older adults, and the resources available to support them. By spreading awareness through community events, educational programs, and media platforms, we can empower individuals to recognize and report abuse, fostering a culture of vigilance and accountability.

Reporting abuse and intervening in suspected cases are crucial steps in protecting our loved ones. We must encourage a society that prioritizes the well-being and safety of older adults by promoting mandatory reporting laws, training professionals to identify abuse, and establishing clear protocols for intervention. By creating a supportive environment that encourages individuals to speak up, we can break the silence surrounding elder abuse and ensure that every case is thoroughly investigated and addressed.

Advocacy is another vital aspect of taking a stand against elder abuse. We must advocate for policy changes that strengthen legal protections, enhance support services, and allocate resources for prevention and intervention initiatives. This requires engaging with policymakers, participating in public consultations, and joining forces with advocacy organizations. Together, we can influence legislation, drive systemic changes, and ensure that elder abuse is a top priority on the public agenda.

Supporting caregivers is integral to addressing elder abuse. Caregivers play a significant role in the lives of older adults, and their well-being directly impacts the quality of care provided. We must advocate for caregiver support programs, access to training and respite care, and recognition of their invaluable contribution. By providing caregivers with the necessary resources and support, we can reduce caregiver stress, prevent burnout, and promote high-quality care for older adults.

Creating a brighter future for our loved ones requires systemic changes in elder care. We must strive for person-centered care that respects the individuality, preferences, and needs of older adults. This includes integrating health and social care services, embracing technological advancements, promoting aging in place, and ensuring a well-trained and supported workforce. Through collaboration among government agencies, healthcare providers, social service organizations, and older adults themselves, we can drive the necessary changes and build an elder care system that truly values and respects the aging population.

In conclusion, the fight against elder abuse is not an easy one, but it is a fight that we must undertake together. It is a fight that demands our unwavering commitment, compassion, and collective action. By taking a stand against elder abuse, we can protect the dignity, well-being, and rights of our loved ones as they age. Let us be the advocates, the caregivers, the policy influencers, and the change agents that our older adults deserve. Together, let us create a future where elder abuse is eradicated, and our loved ones can age with the respect, care, and dignity they deserve.

Recap of Key Insights and Action Points

Throughout this book, we have explored the hidden horrors of elder abuse, exposed its different forms, and discussed strategies for prevention, intervention, and advocacy. As we conclude this journey, it is important to recap the key insights and action points that can guide us in our efforts to address elder abuse effectively. By summarizing these insights and action points, we can reinforce our understanding and commitment to creating a safer and more respectful environment for older adults.

Understanding Elder Abuse
- Elder abuse encompasses various forms, including physical, emotional, sexual, financial, and neglect.

- It is essential to recognize the signs of abuse, such as unexplained injuries, sudden behavioral changes, financial exploitation, and social isolation.

Statistics and Prevalence

- Elder abuse is a widespread problem, affecting millions of older adults worldwide.
- Recognizing the prevalence of abuse underscores the urgency and importance of taking action to prevent and address it.

Factors Contributing to Elder Abuse

- Several factors contribute to the occurrence of elder abuse, including ageism, caregiver stress, social isolation, and lack of awareness and resources.
- Identifying these contributing factors helps us address the root causes and develop targeted interventions.

Recognizing Abuse in Our Loved Ones

- Chapter 2 highlighted the importance of recognizing the signs of abuse, such as physical injuries, emotional distress, sudden changes in behavior, and financial exploitation.
- By being vigilant and observant, we can identify abuse and take appropriate action to protect our loved ones.

Profiles of Abusers

- Understanding the profiles of abusers, including caregivers, family members, and institutional staff, helps us identify potential risks and take preventive measures.

- By recognizing red flags, such as a history of violence, substance abuse, or financial difficulties, we can protect older adults from potential harm.

Exploring Settings Prone to Abuse

- Nursing homes, assisted living facilities, home care agencies, and family dynamics are settings that require heightened attention to prevent abuse.
- Systemic changes, such as stronger regulations, training programs, and improved oversight, are necessary to ensure the safety and well-being of older adults in these settings.

Breaking the Silence

- Encouraging reporting and intervention is crucial to addressing elder abuse effectively.
- Overcoming barriers to reporting, promoting bystander intervention, and ensuring confidentiality and legal protections for whistleblowers are essential action points.

Legal Frameworks and Rights

- Understanding the legal frameworks and rights of older adults helps us advocate for stronger protections and support services.
- Laws and regulations governing elder abuse, guardianship, conservatorship, advance directives, and healthcare decision-making should prioritize the rights and well-being of older adults.

Preventive Measures

- Preventing elder abuse requires education, awareness campaigns, creating a culture of respect and empathy, building strong support networks, and empowering caregivers.

- By focusing on prevention, we can address the underlying factors contributing to abuse and foster a safer environment for older adults.

Healing and Recovery

- Supporting abuse survivors in their physical and emotional recovery is essential.

- Providing counseling, therapy options, and resources for rebuilding trust and restoring dignity can help survivors heal and regain their sense of self-worth.

Advocacy and Policy Changes

- Promoting advocacy efforts and policy changes is vital to combat elder abuse effectively.

- Strengthening elder protection agencies, enhancing law enforcement efforts, and promoting legislative reforms can create a safer and more just society for older adults.

Systemic Changes in Elder Care

- Promoting systemic changes in elder care is necessary to ensure person-centered care, prevent abuse and neglect, integrate health and social care, and support caregivers.

- Workforce development, aging in place, technology and innovation, and policy advocacy are key action points for driving systemic changes.

Addressing elder abuse requires a comprehensive and multi-faceted approach that involves education, awareness, intervention, support, and advocacy. By understanding the key insights and action points summarized above, we can actively contribute to creating a safer and more respectful environment for older adults. Let us take these insights and action points to heart and commit to making a difference in the lives of our loved ones and older adults in our communities. Together, we can work towards a future where elder abuse is eradicated, and all older adults can age with dignity, respect, and the quality of life they deserve.

Encouraging community involvement and engagement

Encouraging community involvement and engagement is crucial in combating elder abuse and creating a supportive environment for older adults. Communities play a vital role in preventing abuse, supporting survivors, and promoting awareness and education. By fostering community involvement, we can strengthen social connections, build a sense of collective responsibility, and empower individuals to take action. In this section, we will explore the importance of community involvement, the benefits it brings, and strategies for encouraging engagement.

Importance of Community Involvement Prevention

Community involvement is essential for preventing elder abuse. By fostering a culture of care, respect, and accountability, communities can create a protective environment for older adults. Community members can watch out for signs of abuse, intervene when necessary, and advocate for preventive measures.

Support

Community involvement provides a vital support network for older adults and their caregivers. It promotes social connections, reduces isolation, and enhances overall well-being. Community members can offer emotional support, practical assistance, and respite care, alleviating the burden on caregivers and creating a sense of belonging for older adults.

Awareness and Education

Engaged communities can raise awareness about elder abuse and promote education initiatives. By organizing workshops, seminars, and community events, they can disseminate information about the signs of abuse, prevention strategies, and available resources. Community members can become ambassadors for change, spreading knowledge and empowering others to take action.

Advocacy

Community involvement strengthens advocacy efforts to address elder abuse at the local, regional, and national levels. Engaged communities can collaborate with advocacy organizations, participate in public consultations, and advocate for policy changes that prioritize the well-being and rights of older adults. They can amplify the collective voice, influence decision-makers, and drive systemic changes.

Benefits of Community Involvement Social Cohesion

Community involvement fosters social cohesion, bringing community members together around a shared cause. It builds a sense of belonging, strengthens social connections, and promotes mutual support and solidarity.

Increased Awareness

Engaged communities raise awareness about elder abuse, ensuring that more people recognize the signs, understand its impact, and know how to respond. This increased awareness creates a vigilant community that is proactive in preventing and addressing elder abuse.

Early Intervention

Communities that are actively involved can detect and intervene in elder abuse cases at an early stage. By encouraging community members to speak up and report suspicions, swift action can be taken to protect older adults and prevent further harm.

Holistic Support

Engaged communities provide holistic support to older adults and their caregivers. They offer practical assistance, emotional support, and access to resources such as counseling services, support groups, and respite care. This support enhances the well-being and quality of life for older adults.

Strategies for Encouraging Community Involvement

Community Partnerships

Foster partnerships between community organizations, local businesses, healthcare providers, faith-based organizations, and advocacy groups. Collaborate on initiatives, share resources, and leverage expertise to address elder abuse collectively.

Community Events and Workshops

Organize community events, workshops, and educational sessions on elder abuse prevention, recognition, and response. Invite guest speakers, experts, and professionals to share their knowledge and provide practical guidance to community members.

Volunteer Programs

Develop volunteer programs that specifically focus on supporting older adults and their caregivers. Recruit and train volunteers to provide companionship, assistance with daily activities, transportation, and respite care. Volunteers can also act as advocates and serve as a source of information and support within the community.

Intergenerational Programs

Create opportunities for intergenerational interaction and engagement. Encourage collaboration between older adults and younger generations through mentorship programs, intergenerational activities, and community projects. This fosters mutual understanding, respect, and appreciation across different age groups.

Neighbourhood Watch Programs

Establish neighbourhood watch programs that include the protection of older adults. Encourage community members to be vigilant and report any suspicious activities or concerns related to the well-being of older adults. Ensure that information on reporting abuse is readily available to all community members.

Community Awareness Campaigns

Launch community-wide awareness campaigns to educate residents about elder abuse. Utilize various channels such as social media, local newspapers, community bulletin boards, and public service announcements to disseminate information, share stories, and promote available resources.

Support Groups

Facilitate support groups for caregivers and older adults who have experienced abuse. These groups provide a safe space for sharing experiences, offering emotional support, and learning from one another. Community members can volunteer to facilitate or provide resources for these groups.

Collaborative Initiatives

Collaborate with local law enforcement agencies, healthcare providers, and social service organizations to develop coordinated responses to elder abuse. Establish protocols for information-sharing, joint investigations, and the provision of support services.

Encouraging community involvement and engagement is essential in combating elder abuse and creating a supportive environment for older adults. By fostering a sense of responsibility, raising awareness, providing support, and promoting advocacy, engaged communities can make a significant impact in preventing and addressing elder abuse. The benefits of community involvement extend beyond the individual level, strengthening social cohesion and creating a society that values and protects its older members. Let us commit to encouraging community involvement, working together to build a safer, more inclusive, and compassionate community for older adults.

Committing to Protect Our Loved Ones and Eradicate Elder Abuse

Elder abuse is a deeply distressing and pervasive issue that affects countless older adults around the world. As we have explored in this book, it is a problem that demands urgent attention and concerted action. To truly make a difference, we must commit to protecting our loved ones and eradicating elder abuse from our society. In this section, we will delve into the importance of this commitment, the actions we can take, and the transformative impact it can have.

Recognizing the Significance of Commitment

Elder abuse thrives in silence and secrecy, often occurring behind closed doors. Committing to protect our loved ones means acknowledging that elder abuse is a serious violation of human rights and a direct threat to the well-being and dignity of older adults. It is a commitment to stand up against abuse, raise awareness, and create a safe and respectful environment for older adults to age with dignity.

Promoting Awareness and Education

Commitment begins with promoting awareness and education. By educating ourselves and others about the signs, risk factors, and consequences of elder abuse, we can recognize and respond to it more effectively. We can engage in conversations with family, friends, and community members, sharing knowledge and resources to create a network of support and vigilance.

Encouraging Open Communication

Commitment to protecting our loved ones involves fostering open communication channels. We must create an environment where older adults feel comfortable discussing their concerns, sharing their experiences, and seeking help without fear of judgment or retribution. By encouraging open dialogue, we can help break the cycle of silence and empower older adults to speak up against abuse.

Building Strong Support Networks

Commitment requires building strong support networks for older adults. This entails connecting with local resources, community organizations, and advocacy groups that specialize in elder abuse prevention and support services. By actively engaging with these networks, we can access information, support survivors, and contribute to the collective effort of eradicating elder abuse.

Reporting Suspected Cases

Committing to protect our loved ones means being proactive in reporting suspected cases of elder abuse. We must overcome our fears and concerns about the potential consequences of reporting, understanding that our actions may save lives and prevent further harm. By reporting abuse to the appropriate authorities, we play a crucial role in breaking the cycle of abuse and ensuring that perpetrators are held accountable.

Advocating for Policy Changes

Commitment extends to advocating for policy changes that strengthen legal protections and support services for older adults. We can engage in grassroots advocacy efforts, contacting local representatives, participating in public consultations, and joining forces with advocacy organizations. By amplifying our collective voice, we can influence policy decisions, drive legislative reforms, and create a more robust framework for elder abuse prevention and intervention.

Supporting Caregivers

Recognizing the important role caregivers play in the lives of older adults, commitment includes supporting and empowering them. Caregiver burnout and stress can contribute to elder abuse, so providing respite care, education, and emotional support is vital. By advocating for caregiver support programs and resources, we contribute to the overall well-being of older adults and help create healthier caregiving environments.

Challenging Ageism and Stereotypes

Commitment to protecting our loved ones requires challenging ageism and stereotypes that perpetuate elder abuse. We must foster a society that values and respects older adults, celebrating their wisdom, experiences, and contributions. By promoting positive narratives and challenging ageist attitudes, we can create a culture that treats older adults with dignity and ensures their protection.

Embracing Intergenerational Connection

Commitment involves fostering intergenerational connections and understanding. By fostering interactions between older adults and younger generations, we can break down barriers, foster empathy, and create a sense of interdependence. Through shared experiences and mutual respect, we can build a society that values the well-being of all its members.

Continual Learning and Improvement

Commitment to protecting our loved ones and eradicating elder abuse requires continual learning and improvement. We must stay informed about evolving best practices, research findings, and emerging trends in elder abuse prevention and intervention. By actively seeking new knowledge and challenging our own biases, we can adapt our approaches and make a greater impact in protecting older adults.

Committing to protect our loved ones and eradicating elder abuse is a moral imperative and a collective responsibility. It requires active engagement, awareness, education, and advocacy. By promoting awareness, encouraging open communication, building support networks, reporting suspected cases, advocating for policy changes, supporting caregivers, challenging ageism, embracing intergenerational connections, and fostering continual learning, we can make a transformative difference in the lives of older adults. Let us stand united in our commitment, working tirelessly to create a society where older adults are valued, respected, and protected from the horrors of elder abuse. Together, we can build a future where every older adult can age with dignity, safety, and the love they deserve.

Conclusión

En esta exploración exhaustiva del abuso a los ancianos, hemos arrojado luz sobre los horrores ocultos que enfrentan los adultos mayores y discutido estrategias para proteger a nuestros seres queridos y construir un futuro libre de abuso a los ancianos. A lo largo de este libro, hemos profundizado en las diferentes formas de abuso a los ancianos, examinado los factores que contribuyen a su ocurrencia, resaltado la importancia de reconocer las señales y explorado los perfiles de los abusadores. También hemos discutido la prevalencia del abuso a los ancianos, los marcos legales existentes y los cambios sistémicos necesarios para crear un entorno más seguro para los adultos mayores. Ahora, al concluir este viaje, nos encontramos con una comprensión profunda de la necesidad urgente de abordar este problema persistente.

El abuso a los ancianos es un problema profundamente preocupante que afecta a millones de adultos mayores en todo el mundo. Representa una violación de los derechos humanos, erosiona la dignidad y socava el bienestar de nuestra población en envejecimiento. Es imperativo que actuemos para proteger a nuestros seres queridos y crear una sociedad donde los adultos mayores puedan vivir con seguridad, respeto y la calidad de vida que merecen.

A lo largo de los capítulos de este libro, hemos obtenido conocimientos valiosos sobre el abuso a los ancianos. Hemos aprendido sobre las diferentes formas que puede tomar, incluyendo el abuso físico, emocional, sexual, financiero y negligente. Hemos examinado los factores complejos que contribuyen a su ocurrencia, como el edadismo, el estrés de los cuidadores, el aislamiento social y la falta de conciencia y recursos. Al comprender las diversas facetas del abuso a los ancianos, estamos mejor preparados para abordar el problema de manera directa.

Reconocer las señales del abuso a los ancianos es de suma importancia. Hemos discutido los indicadores físicos y conductuales que pueden indicar abuso, como lesiones inexplicables, cambios repentinos en el comportamiento, explotación financiera y aislamiento social. Al estar alerta y ser proactivos en el reconocimiento de estas señales, podemos intervenir y tomar las medidas necesarias para proteger a nuestros seres queridos.

En la lucha contra el abuso a los ancianos, la colaboración y la participación comunitaria son esenciales. Las familias, las comunidades, las organizaciones y los formuladores de políticas tienen un papel que desempeñar en la prevención y el abordaje del abuso a los ancianos. Las familias deben fomentar la comunicación abierta, brindar apoyo emocional y crear un entorno en el que los adultos mayores se sientan seguros para compartir sus preocupaciones. Las comunidades pueden crear conciencia, establecer redes de apoyo y crear una cultura que valore y respete a los adultos mayores. Las organizaciones y los formuladores de políticas deben priorizar el desarrollo y la implementación de estrategias integrales, leyes y regulaciones para proteger a los adultos mayores contra el abuso y garantizar su bienestar.

Los esfuerzos legislativos desempeñan un papel crucial en la lucha contra el abuso a los ancianos. Los gobiernos deben promulgar y hacer cumplir leyes que aborden específicamente el abuso a los ancianos, brinden protecciones legales y asignen recursos para la prevención, la intervención y los servicios de apoyo. Las leyes de denuncia obligatoria, las verificaciones exhaustivas de antecedentes para los cuidadores y los mecanismos estrictos de supervisión son pasos cruciales para crear un entorno más seguro para los adultos mayores.

Los cambios sistémicos dentro del sistema de atención a los ancianos son necesarios para abordar las causas fundamentales del abuso a los ancianos. Debemos esforzarnos por brindar atención centrada en la persona, integrar servicios de salud y sociales, invertir en el apoyo y la formación de los cuidadores y mejorar los mecanismos de supervisión y monitoreo. Al fomentar un enfoque holístico y compasivo hacia el cuidado de los ancianos, podemos crear un entorno que proteja el bienestar y la dignidad de los adultos mayores.

La educación y la conciencia son fundamentales en la lucha contra el abuso a los ancianos. Al difundir información, llevar a cabo campañas de concienciación y promover iniciativas educativas, podemos capacitar a individuos, familias, cuidadores y comunidades para reconocer y prevenir el abuso a los ancianos. Los programas de capacitación para profesionales y cuidadores pueden equiparlos con el conocimiento y las habilidades necesarias para brindar cuidados compasivos y éticos.

En resumen, "Horrores Ocultos: Exponiendo el Abuso a los Ancianos y Protegiendo a Nuestros Seres Queridos" es un llamado a la acción. Nos insta a unirnos en la lucha contra el abuso a los ancianos y trabajar juntos para crear un mundo donde los adultos mayores puedan envejecer con dignidad, respeto y el amor que merecen. Tomemos medidas ahora y seamos parte de la solución. Permitamos que la luz ilumine los horrores ocultos del abuso a los ancianos y creemos un mundo donde nuestros seres queridos mayores estén seguros, valorados y protegidos.

www.ingramcontent.com/pod-product-compliance
Lightning Source LLC
LaVergne TN
LVHW061528070526
838199LV00009B/421